YELLOWSTONE

TRAILS

*A Hiking
Guide*

MARK C. MARSCHALL

The Yellowstone Association for Natural Science, History & Education, Inc.

1990

Published by: The Yellowstone Association
               Box 117
               Yellowstone National Park, WY 82190

Printed by: Maverick Publications
             Bend, Oregon

Layout: Kelly Steers

Cover Design: Mark Marschall
               Gary Asher

Photographs and illustrations by author unless otherwise noted.

Library of Congress Number: 90-070639

ISBN 0-89288-197-6

CONTENTS

PREFACE

This new edition of *Yellowstone Trails* has been completely revised after the fires of 1988. Information on burned areas, trail reroutes and new trails has been added. There are new sections on water treatment, backcountry camping, and bear attacks. Photographs and topographic maps have also been added. And of course there is the flashy cover, which represents some of the new color patterns in Yellowstone—the black of the burned trees, the bright green of the new grass, and the violet color of the fireweed which blooms in the burned areas. This is all quite a change from the book as it originally appeared in 1978.

Back in 1978, after 6 summers of hiking in the park, I wrote the first edition of *Yellowstone Trails*. At the time I thought I knew quite a bit about Yellowstone's backcountry. I was wrong. With 12 more years of experience in Yellowstone behind me, much of it as a backcountry ranger, I can see now that I had only scratched the surface of backcountry lore. Although I'm probably still only scratching the surface, I have learned a lot in those years, both from other people and from what I've seen myself.

One of the things I've learned is how important and special Yellowstone is—and how fragile. The crush of civilization is expanding everywhere, yet you can still escape it by hiking back into this huge piece of untamed country, country filled with wild animals, mountains, rivers, lakes, hot springs and geysers. We must keep Yellowstone wild by travelling lightly in the backcountry, limiting our impacts on the plants, animals, and geologic features. Harm is easy to cause and hard to undo. We can start by following the park's regulations, but even this is not enough. We much act with a conscience and consider the effects of our own actions in the backcountry. Treat Yellowstone as if you have a stake in it's future, because you do.

I've also learned that the wild quality that makes Yellowstone special can be dangerous to those that come in contact with it. As a park ranger, I've seen first hand the fatal consequences of making a mistake or just being in the wrong place at the wrong time in the backcountry. Some people feel that because this is a national park they are protected from danger. This of course is wrong. Even with all the rules, regulations, and rangers, Yellowstone is full of hazards; it's up to you to keep yourself safe. It is true that accidents and fatalities are few and far between. And many people have hiked here for years with not so much as a sprained ankle, but that doesn't mean we can get complacent. All I ask is that you be aware of the danger, and temper your actions in the backcountry with some caution. At the end of this book is a list of names. The people on this list were all killed in the last decade while on backcountry trips in Yellowstone. This list is a memorial to them and a reminder to us.

There is a certain amount of responsibility that comes with writing a trail guide and I have always worried about the consequences of people buying my book and using it to guide them on a hike through Yellowstone. I worry about people hurting themselves or hurting the park while on a backcountry trip inspired by this book—hence the cautionary tone of the previous two paragraphs. What makes this worrying bearable (besides my "huge" royalty checks) is that for the last decade or so, people have been using this book to get them started on some very enjoyable hikes, hikes they may remember for the rest of their lives. I hope that attribute continues with this edition, and that this book will help you experience all the good things Yellowstone's backcountry has to offer.

MCM
Yellowstone Lake, Wyoming

HOW TO USE THIS GUIDE

Yellowstone National Park's backcountry covers over 2 million acres and contains over 1,000 miles of trails. It is hard for most of us to comprehend such a large, wild area. Not surprisingly, it is also hard to choose which trail to hike. Unless, of course, you use this book.

Start with the Pre-Hike section. First is a listing of suggested hikes, ingeniously divided into short, medium and long categories. This will give you trail names, distances and page numbers so that you can look up and read the specific trail descriptions. Next comes a map of Yellowstone, which shows you how the park is divided up into areas and maps. If you want to hike in a specific area look at the Yellowstone map to find out the page number of the specific map for that area. Use the index at the back of the book if you only know the name of the place you want to go.

Next comes a variety of general information that may help you choose a trail, as well as make your hiking safer and more enjoyable. A concern of most hikers is the effect of the fires of 1988. Another major concern is grizzly bears. Both of these topics are covered in the Pre-Hike section. Also covered are backcountry permits, hiking equipment, wildlife viewing, petrified forests, thermal features, stream crossings, weather, maps, and water treatment.

Following the Pre-Hike Section are the specific trail descriptions for 116 different trails, and 23 topographic maps.

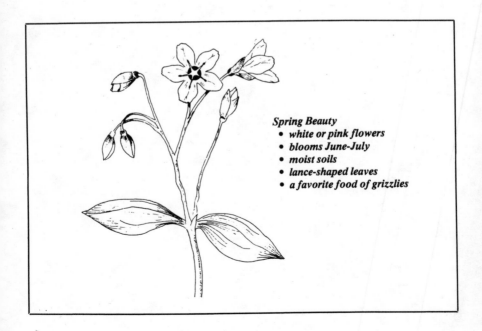

Spring Beauty
- *white or pink flowers*
- *blooms June-July*
- *moist soils*
- *lance-shaped leaves*
- *a favorite food of grizzlies*

YELLOWSTONE NATIONAL PARK
BACKCOUNTRY REGULATIONS

The following are paraphrased from their legal origin in the Code of Federal Regulations. For a complete list of the regulations, contact the National Park Service.

All overnight trips into the backcountry require a Backcountry Use Permit.

No firearms or weapons allowed.

No pets allowed. Horses, mules and llamas are the only domestic animals allowed.

All trash must be packed out.

Only dead and down timber may be used for firewood.

Don't feed or harass animals.

No collecting any rock specimens, antlers, or bones of animals.

Do not disturb any cultural or prehistoric artifacts.

All food, when not in use, must be stored out of reach of bears.

No dumping any waste within 100 feet of any stream or other body of water. No dish washing allowed in any body of water.

A free permit and knowledge of the rules are required for fishing.

Fires are allowed only in established fire rings.

No bathing, washing dishes, or cooking in thermal features.

Gathering nuts, berries, mushrooms, etc., for personal consumption is allowed.

Backcountry patrol cabins are strictly for official use. Breaking into one of these in other than a life and death emergency is prohibited.

Throughout this guide you will notice that certain trails have this logo:

This logo signifies a bear management area.

These trails travel through areas that have scheduled closures or restrictions on their use during certain times of the year. This is an attempt by the National Park Service to allow bears undisturbed use of prime habitat. A list and map of the scheduled closures is available by mail from the National Park Service, Box 168, Yellowstone N.P., WY 82190, or at any ranger station.

SHORT HIKES

	Roundtrip Distance		Page No.
Starting from the Mammoth Area:			
Bunsen Peak	4 miles	6.5 km	54
Osprey Falls	4	6.5	54
Beaver Ponds Loop	5	8	55
Grizzly Lake	4	6.5	46
Rescue Creek Trail	8*	13*	61
Starting from the Tower Area:			
Tower Falls Trail	1	1.6	64
Lost Lake Loop	4	6.5	65
Yellowstone River Picnic Area Tr.	4	6.5	64
Mt. Washburn	6	9.6	90
Starting from Northeast Entrance Road:			
Slough Creek Trail (to first meadows)	4	6.5	70
Lamar Trail (to Cache Creek)	6.2	10	74
Pebble Creek Trail (to upper meadows from Warm Creek)	4	6.5	72
Starting from Canyon Area:			
Grebe Lake	6	9.6	93
Cascade Lake (from picnic area)	4.4	7	95
Mt. Washburn	6	9.6	90
Starting from Norris Area:			
Solfatara Creek Trail (first 3 miles)	6	9.6	97
Norris Campground to Ice Lake T.H.	4.5*	7*	97
Artist Paint Pot	1	1.6	98
Starting from Lake/Bridge Bay/ Fishing Bridge Area:			
Elephant Back Loop	4	6.5	104
Storm Point Loop	2	3	86
Avalanche Peak Trail	4	6.5	153
Starting from Grant Village/ Lewis Lake Area:			
Riddle Lake	4	6.5	122
Dogshead Trail to Shoshone Lake	8	13	122
Starting from Old Faithful Area:			
Mystic Falls	2	3	110
Fairy Falls	5	8	110
Lone Star Geyser	5	8	115
Observation Point	2	3	116
Starting from Madison Area:			
Purple Mountain	6	10	105

*These distances are one way, starting from one trailhead and coming out at another.

MEDIUM DISTANCE HIKES

	Roundtrip Distance		Page No.
Starting from Mammoth Area:			
Sepulcher Mountain Loop	12 miles	19 km	*56*
Electric Peak	17	27	*53*
Fawn Pass	24	38.5	*49*
Bighorn Pass	16	25.5	*48*
Mt. Holmes	20	32	*47*
Blacktail T.H. to Knowles Falls	10.5	16.8	*61*
Blacktail T.H. to Hellroaring T.H.	14*	22.5*	*59*
Starting from Tower Area:			
Garnet Hill Loop	7.5	12	*68*
Specimen Ridge Trail	17.5*	28*	*69*
(Yellowstone Riv. P.A. to Lamar TH)			
Yellowstone River Trail	20.5*	33*	*59*
(Tower R.S. to Gardiner)			
Starting from Northeast Entrance Road:			
Bliss Pass	20.6*	33*	*72*
(Pebble Ck. C.G. to Slough C.G.)			
Pebble Creek Trail	12*	19.2*	*72*
(Pebble Ck. C.G. to Warm Creek)			
Republic Pass	17*	27*	*78*
(Thunderer Cutoff to Cooke City)			
Starting from Canyon Area:			
Mt. Washburn	11.5*	18.5*	*91*
(Dunraven Pass to Glacial Boulder)			
7-Mile Hole	11	17.5	*93*
Howard Eaton Trail	10.5*	17*	*95*
(Cascade Lake Trl. to Ice Lake)			
Observation Peak	11	17.5	*95*
Starting from Lake/Bridge Bay Area:			
Pelican Valley loop	15.5	25	*83*
Park Point	13	21	*148*
Starting from Grant Village/Lewis Lake/ South Entrance Area:			
Heart Lake	16	26	*138*
Heart Lake Trail to South Entrance	23.5*	38*	*138*
Mt. Sheridan	23.5	38	*139*
Shoshone Lake Loop	11	17.5	*122*
(Lewis Channel Trl. to Dogshead Trl.)			
Union Falls	14	22.4	*128*

* These distances are one way, starting from one trailhead and coming out at another.

MEDIUM DISTANCE HIKES

	Roundtrip Distance		Page No.
Starting from Old Faithful Area:			
Shoshone Lake via Lone Star Geyser	17 miles	27 km	*120*
Fairy Creek Trail	13.5	21.6	*114*
Mallard Lake Loop	11.8	19	*116*
Starting from West Entrance/			
Gallatin Highway (U.S. 191) Area:			
Gneiss Creek Trail	14*	22.5*	*107*
Skyline Trail Loop	20.5	32.8	*41*
Sportsman Lake	22	35	*43*
Crescent Lake/High Lake Loop	22	35	*42*
Starting from Bechler Area:			
Dunanda Falls	18	28.8	*127*
Bechler River Trail			
(Cave Falls to 3 Rivers Jct.)	29.6	47.4	*126*
Union Falls (Cave Falls to Union Falls)	23	37	*129*

*These distances are one way, starting from one trailhead and coming out at another.

LONG HIKES

	Roundtrip Distance		Page No.
Fawn Pass-Fan Creek-Electric Pass Loop:			
Starting from Glen Creek Trailhead	43 miles	69 km	*55, 50*
Starting from Trailhead at Milepost 22	42	67	
Pelican Valley-Lamar Valley	33	53	*85, 74*
(Pelican Trailhead to Lamar Trailhead)			
Hoodoo Basin	57	91	*79*
(Lamar Trailhead to Hoodoo Basin and			
park boundary back to Lamar T.H.)			
Pelican Valley-Frost Lake-Pahaska Lodge	35.5	57	*80, 85*
Heart Lake-South Boundary-Snake River			
Loop	56.5	90.5	*138-144*
(Heart Lake T.H. to Snake River Trail			
to South Boundary Trail to Harebell Jct. to			
Heart Lake to Heart Lake T.H.)			
Thorofare Trail-Two Ocean Plateau Loop	80	128	*148-151*
(9-mile Trailhead to Thorofare R.S. to			
Two Ocean Plateau Trail to Trail Creek			
Trail to 9-mile Trailhead)			
Bechler River-Shoshone Lake-Old Faithful	34	54.5	*126*
(Cave Falls to Bechler River Trail to			
Shoshone Lake to Lone Star Trailhead at			
Old Faithful)			

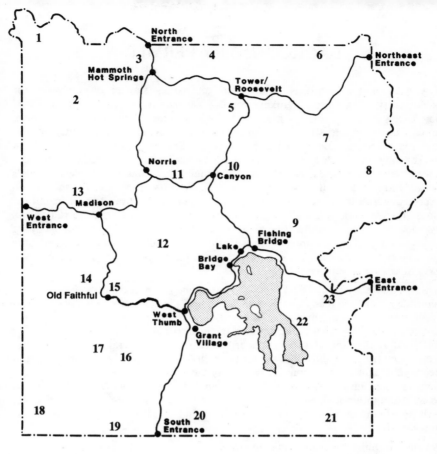

BACKCOUNTRY PERMITS

A backcountry permit is required of all parties staying overnight in the backcountry. If you are day hiking you don't generally need a permit. (Off-trail day hiking in some areas, such as the Washburn Range and Two Ocean Plateau may require a permit. Check at a ranger station for details.) Backcountry permits are free of charge and available from Ranger Stations and Visitor Centers. A backcountry permit does two things: it reserves a backcountry campsite for you and it lets the rangers know your trip itinerary. Camping in Yellowstone's backcountry is done at designated campsites. When you get your permit, you'll choose at which campsites you will stay for which nights of your trip. If one of the campsites you choose has already been reserved by someone else, the ranger will ask you to choose another site as a substitute. Once you have your campsite reserved on your backcountry permit, you'll be assured of having a spot at those campsites. And because most campsites are one party sites, your hiking group will have those sites to yourselves.

If it sounds as if the Park Service is running the backcountry like a motel, remember there are many people wanting to use the campsites. By keeping areas from becoming overcrowded and overused the Park Service is ensuring the preservation of the backcountry and a quality experience for those that venture into it. If all the campsites in an area are taken you have several other alternatives. You may want to day hike into the area (which doesn't require a permit). You may delay your hike until a campsite is available; campsites can be reserved no more than 48 hours ahead of time, so your wait won't be a long one. Or you may decide to hike in another area where the sites are more available. The system works very well for the majority of the hikers and you'll find that it isn't nearly as confusing as it sounds.

One last thing, it's a good idea to sign in at the trailhead register at the start of your hike. If you are overdue and rangers see that you have actually signed in at the register, then they can narrow their search to that backcountry area. This is especially important for day hikers.

DAY HIKING AND BACKPACKING EQUIPMENT

The two most popular methods of exploring Yellowstone's backcountry are day hiking and backpacking. Day hiking simply means starting and returning on a hike the same day. Backpacking refers to hiking into the backcountry and camping for one or several nights.

By day hiking you can avoid buying and carrying a lot of expensive equipment. In fact, you probably already own the essential items needed for summer day hiking in Yellowstone. The basic hiking wardrobe starts with a pair of comfortable walking shoes. When I started hiking here, heavy, leather, mountaineering boots were the only acceptable footwear for the serious Yellowstone hiker. They took a couple years to break in, caused blisters, and doubled in weight when they got wet. What more could you want in footwear? Now thankfully, running shoes and light weight nylon and leather hiking shoes are the footwear of choice for day hikers. These shoes don't offer much protection from moisture, but they are so comfortable and light, that the trade off is worth it. My only recommendation is that if you use running shoes, use those that have a lug sole tread design for better traction. To the shoes, add a pair of loose, comfortable pants, preferably made of a material that isn't very water absorbent—something that dries quickly. Nylon running pants, cotton/nylon blend pants, or light wool pants are much better than jeans. Many people hike in shorts and only put the pants on if they get cool. A t-shirt, supplemented with a jersey made of pile or polypropylene-type fabric, or a wool sweater gives you a flexible outfit. (Obviously during cooler weather you'll need some extra clothing). You'll also need a small daypack or knapsack, or a fanny pack, to carry the "essentials" which are:

—*A raincoat, poncho or parka. Remember it can rain anytime no matter what the forecast said.*

—*A warm hat. It'll keep your head dry and prevent heat loss through your head if you should get cold.*

—*A water bottle. Any plastic container that doesn't leak will do.*

—*Insect repellent (needed between mid June and late August).*

—*Sunscreen. Wrinkles and weather-beaten skin are no longer trendy. Skin cancer never was.*

—*A first aid kit suited to your needs.*

These items will get you comfortably through most short summer day hikes. For longer day hikes consider taking: a map, compass, Swiss army knife, and matches. An overnight hike obviously requires all the above equipment and then some. Before taking your first overnight backcountry trip it will be well worth your while to look through one of the many books dealing with backpacking equipment, techniques and food (see appendix). The following section of this guide will deal just with the essentials for backpacking in Yellowstone.

For an overnight hike in Yellowstone you'll need to bring some extra warm clothing and a sleeping bag suitable for the expected night time temperatures (see Weather section). A shelter of some sort is a must. A tarp is nice and light, but in a blowing rain or during biting-insect season a tent can be worth every ounce of extra weight. 100 feet of cord or rope, and a stuff sack for hanging food and garbage will also be needed (see Camping section). For cooking, a backpacking stove is required at some of Yellowstone's campsites, and is generally a good idea anywhere because of its ability to cook even when it's raining or snowing and dry firewood is scarce. Fires are allowed in the fire rings at many backcountry campsites, but usable firewood is becoming scarce near some of these sites. In collecting wood for a fire, remember that regulations allow only down timber to be used. No chopping down live or standing dead trees, or breaking off branches of either, is allowed. A small backpack saw can come in handy for cutting up large logs at sites where small firewood is scarce.

BACKCOUNTRY CAMPING

Camping in Yellowstone's backcountry allows you to experience the park on a much more intimate level than does day hiking. And the more days you're out, the deeper that intimacy becomes. The feeling that comes from sitting at camp and watching the landscape around you change from evening to night, and dawn change to day, transcends my limited descriptive vocabulary. To fully appreciate Yellowstone's backcountry, you must go out overnight.

Of course bears will be on your mind. And rightfully so. But you can reduce your worrying by using good camping technique. Good camping technique starts when you arrive at your campsite. Look the area over for any sign of bear activity (see Coexisting with Bears section) and check for any animal trails (call them "game trails" and you'll sound more knowledgeable) running through the camping area. If you see evidence of recent bear activity in the campsite, do not camp there. You do not want to risk having the bear revisit the campsite while you are there. Move to another campsite even if you're tired. Rangers check backcountry campsites periodically and close them if there is bear activity, or if other hikers have reported bears in that camp. This keeps your chance of being given a permit for a campsite with recent bear activity to a minimum.

Next, set up your tent as far away as possible from the cooking area, food storage tree, main trail, or any game trails. 100 yards is not too far, but local topography may limit the distance to less than that. (see diagram) Bears routinely use trails at night, and in the unlikely event that a bear investigates your camp, it will probably be drawn to the areas with the strongest food odors. If you keep your sleeping area food-odor free, and away from the above areas, you will greatly reduce the chance of having a bear visit your tent.

14

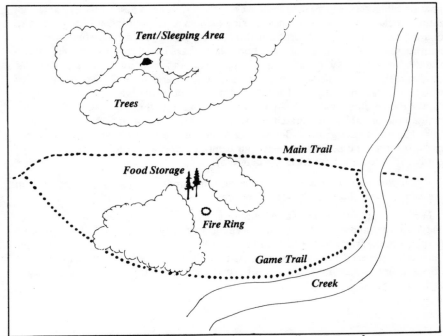

Place sleeping area as far as possible from trails, streams and cooking/food storage area.

Do all your cooking and food preparation at the fire ring/cooking area. Keep food odors to a minimum. Avoid frying foods. Freeze dried food or meals cooked in plastic bags are especially handy and allow for easier clean-up. Clean dishes immediately after eating. If fires are allowed at your campsite, burn any garbage from the meal, but make sure the fire is hot enough to burn it completely. Pick any unburned garbage or food out of the fire and put it in your trash bag before you go to sleep. If you cooked a particularly odorous meal, you should consider changing clothes. Washing after your meal is also a good idea. And most importantly, before you go to sleep, you must store your food and garbage out of reach of bears.

In most campsites in Yellowstone the National Park Service has put up either a pole or cable between trees to be used for food storage. These poles or cables are usually located near the fire ring/cooking area so as to concentrate food odors to one spot in the campsite. Store your food in one sealed plastic bag, your garbage in another sealed plastic bag, then put both plastic bags into a nylon stuff sack (which should be used only as a food storage sack and not for your sleeping bag afterwards). Take a piece of 50 foot cord or rope and tie some weight (piece of wood or rock) to one end. Throw that end of the rope over the pole or cable. Lower the weighted end back down to the ground. Position the rope in the middle of the pole or cable, then attach the stuff sack and hoist it up. Make sure it is at least 10 feet off the ground. Tie the other end of the rope off around one of the trees. If there is no pole or cable at your campsite, you will need an extra 50 feet of cord or rope to hang your food (see diagram).

When you leave your campsite make sure the fire is out, pick out any foil from the ashes and any litter left behind in the area.

For disposing of human waste, choose a spot at least 100 feet away from any water source, and away from your sleeping area. Dig a small hole between 4-8″ deep, place the waste in the hole and cover it back over with the extra dirt. Do not burn toilet paper at the waste site unless there is no fire danger, instead burn it at the campfire pit. Do not attempt to bury any extra food or garbage as bears will just dig it up.

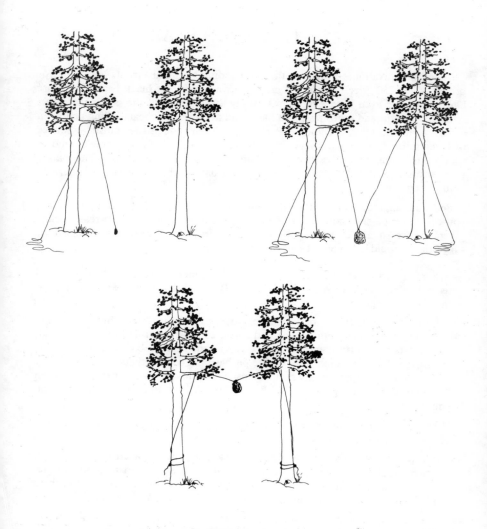

HANGING FOOD

1. *Pick two trees about 20-25 feet apart.*

2. *Go to one tree and throw the end of a 50 foot piece of rope over a branch that is at least 17 feet off the ground.*

3. *Go to the other tree and do the same with another 50 foot piece of rope.*

4. *Attach food bag to the ends of both ropes.*

5. *Pull ropes tight so that food bag is equidistant between the two trees. Take as much of the sag out of the ropes as possible and make sure the food bag is at least 12 feet off the ground.*

6. *Tie ropes off at the base of the trees.*

COEXISTING WITH BEARS

Yellowstone National Park and the surrounding National Forests are home for probably 200-250 grizzly bears and an unknown number of black bears (bears are hard to see and even harder to count). Many hikers know of the bear's incredible strength, stealth, and craftiness, and have read about grizzly bears killing people in Yellowstone and Glacier National Park. Thus, even though the statistical chance of being injured by a bear is very small, it is at the front of most people's mind as they are travelling in the backcountry. And that is good, to an extent. The danger from bears is real. You cannot eliminate the danger, but you can considerably reduce it by your actions.

Bears are unpredictable. Although seeing one in the backcountry is a great thrill, you can never be sure how the bear will react if it sees you. For this reason most hikers prefer to avoid meeting bears in the first place. The following list of suggestions should help you prevent such an encounter.

—Ask at a Visitor Center or Ranger Station if there have been bears spotted recently along the trail you wish to hike. Also check for posted warning signs at the trailhead register.

—Once on the trail, check for recent bear tracks and scat. If you find fresh sign, especially many tracks going back and forth, consider returning to the trailhead. At your backcountry campsite, check for recent sign of bears including scat, tracks, and any indication that the fire pit has been scattered about or dug up by a bear. Avoid camping at any such campsite and move to another campsite, even if it's not the one assigned to you. Report all bear sign to a ranger station when you return.

—Hike in a group of 4 or more people. This seems to greatly lessen the chance of a bear encounter or attack.

—Avoid perfumes and strong deodorants. Bears may be attracted to these odors. Women should be aware that their scent during menstruation may also attract bears; but this has not been proven conclusively one way or the other, and there is no record of bears being provoked into such an attack in Yellowstone.

—Make noise to keep from surprising a bear. They will usually leave an area if they know you're coming. Although the constant ringing of a bell, rattling of a rock in a can, or the off key singing of your companion will warn a bear of your presence, it may also take a good deal of the enjoyment out of hiking. Thus it will usually suffice to only make the noises intermittently, being sure to ring, rattle, or sing well in advance of any blind spots on the trail.

—Don't hike at night. Bears often use the trails after dark.

—Use proper camping techniques (see Camping Section).

The previous suggestions should greatly reduce the chance of meeting a black or a grizzly bear. But in spite of these precautions, you may still encounter a bear on your backcountry trip. These people-bear encounters usually fit into one of 3 broad categories:

1) Spotting a bear from a distance; bear may or may not see you.

2) Close encounter, often involving a charge, possibly an attack.

3) Bear coming into your campsite.

I'll discuss these situations one at a time, realizing that in an actual encounter they may overlap. You should also realize that there are no absolutes when dealing with bears. Each bear has a different personality, and the same situation may cause one bear to attack while another flees. (Grizzlies do seem to be more aggressive than black bears). Even though there have been many bear encounters and attacks in North America from which to draw inferences on bear behavior, it is difficult to make conclusions due to the incredible number of variables that are part of each incident. I have drawn on numerous sources (see appendix), including my own experience in investigating bear incidents and observing bears in Yellowstone, for the following information and suggestions. In some situations, where there is no clear-cut, proven-reliable course of action I have presented what I would do, or have done, in that situation. But no course of action is guaranteed to work every time. This is just part of the inherent risk with travelling in grizzly country.

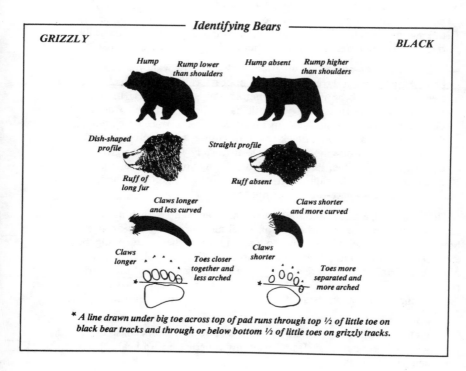

—— Identifying Bears ——

GRIZZLY

BLACK

Hump | Rump lower than shoulders | Hump absent | Rump higher than shoulders

Dish-shaped profile | Straight profile

Ruff of long fur | Ruff absent

Claws longer and less curved | Claws shorter and more curved

Claws longer | Toes closer together and less arched | Claws shorter | Toes more separated and more arched

* A line drawn under big toe across top of pad runs through top ½ of little toe on black bear tracks and through or below bottom ½ of little toes on grizzly tracks.

The first type of encounter, **viewing the bear from a distance,** might occur while you are hiking in or near a large open area and see a bear feeding or walking about 100-200 yards away, and the bear apparently hasn't yet sensed your presence. This is the most common type of bear encounter in Yellowstone's backcountry.

— If the bear hasn't seen you, turn around and slowly go back the way you came. Leave this trail to hike another day. If you choose to detour around the bear, give it as wide of a berth as possible. Move to cover and watch the bear to determine its direction of travel and choose your detour accordingly. If it is a grizzly sow with cubs, I would not try a detour if it was possible to go back the way I came.

— There is probably no reason to draw attention to yourself in such an encounter. If you can leave the area without the bear knowing you were there, all the better. Thus, running or quick motions are probably a bad idea. It also appears as if bears have a tendency, as do other predators, to chase things that run from them.

— If the bear senses (smells, hears, or sees) you from a distance, it often will leave the area. Although some bears, those that have become habituated to human presence, may know you are nearby but will exhibit no outward reaction.

— If the bear senses you from a distance and starts advancing slowly, or stands up, it is probably trying to determine what manner of creature it has sensed. The correct response to this situation is not clear. It may be of benefit to help the bear identify you by waving your arms, talking in an even voice, and moving up wind of the bear. Hopefully once the bear has identified you as a human it will then leave the area.

— In the above non-aggressive situations with a grizzly bear, you can also be looking for a good tree to climb. It appears as if the time to climb a tree is before a bear is upset or before the bear charges. In other words, climb the tree while you still have plenty of time to do so. Grizzly bears have gone high up into trees after people by climbing limb over limb as we do. (Black bears, of course, can climb just about any tree). If you do climb a tree, get at least 17 feet off the ground, and higher if possible. Remember that injuring yourself by falling out of a tree, or by being pulled out, may be just as dangerous as another course of action where you choose not to climb.

The second type of situation is a **close range encounter,** such as coming around the bend of a trail or over the rise of a hill and surprising a bear at close range. Some habituated bears may just go back to what they were doing before you surprised them, but most bears will eventually either flee, bluff charge, or attack. No one is certain of the correlations between your actions and the bear's response to them, or if there even is one. It does appear as if a grizzly sow with cubs is more likely to charge than a lone bear. Also, it is not unusual for a lone bear to flee.

— I would stand my ground and let the bear make the first move. Hopefully it will flee. I would not run, as I've seen bears chase down much faster animals than I; and from my experience with bears, I feel running incites them.

— If the bear charges, it may stop the charge a few feet in front of you (bluff charge) or the charge may continue into an attack. Many people have avoided injury while standing their ground. They may shout, talk softly, stay quiet or throw something to distract the bear; many combinations have worked. The advantage of standing your ground, instead of running, is that it allows you to watch the bear through the entire charge and to respond appropriately.

— In cases in Yellowstone where a bear has charged and stopped right in front of a person, a detrimental action seems to be pushing, hitting, or kicking the bear. In these instances the bears responded by biting or clawing the person. If I had a bear stop a charge right in front of me, I would stay still, talk softly to it, and hope that it would turn away. I would try to not look it in the eye. If I made a movement or action that seemed to incite the bear, I would not do it again. If the bear moved away, I would stay still until it was out of sight or at least 100 yards away. At least that is what I would try to do.

— When the bear continues the charge into an attack, either just before or just after the bear hits, you should play dead. This drastic action has worked dozens of times in apparently limiting injuries during a bear attack. In past attacks in Yellowstone it has appeared as if fighting back or movement prolongs the attack, and only after resistance has stopped does the attack cease. A reasonable theory is that the bear charges and attacks during a surprise encounter because you are perceived as a threat by the bear. The bear attacks out of defense. As long as you fight, or show signs of life, you remain a threat to the bear.

— To play dead: Lay on your stomach. Interlock your fingers over the back of your neck and bring your elbows up to cover your face. Your pack offers protection for your back, leaving only your buttocks and legs exposed. The bear may bite and scratch you, but you must remain still and silent. This sounds incredibly difficult, but many "ordinary" people have done it. In talking to people who have played dead and been bitten and scratched by a grizzly, they have told me that they weren't aware of any pain during the attack. Once the bear leaves you, don't move, as the bear may be watching you from a short ways off, looking for signs of life. Continue listening and only move when you are sure the bear has left the area.

The third type of incident is **when a bear comes into your campsite** or prowls around the perimeter of the camping area. This usually happens at night and is, potentially, a very dangerous situation. A bear that willingly comes this close to people has probably had a past association with people and our food. This is a much different situation than surprising a bear at close range and having the bear react defensively. This type of bear is probably after food and may even, in rare circumstances, view you as prey. This is the type of situation where a chemical repellent might be useful.

— If the bear enters the camping area while you are up and about you should retreat slowly from the bear, possibly throwing down things to distract the bear. Watch the bear as you retreat. Consider climbing a tree in this situation, as there is no campsite in Yellowstone without trees nearby. If and when the bear leaves the area, do not go to sleep or move camp a short distance and try to sleep there. If you feel the bear is still nearby, stay in the tree, all night if you have to. When you get back to the trailhead, report this type of incident to rangers immediately so they may close the campsite and prevent others from having the same experience.

— If the bear enters the camping area while you are asleep and pulls you or one of your party out of the tent, this is the time to fight back. Do not play dead in this situation. This is one of those extremely rare situations which have occurred periodically in Yellowstone and other areas in bear country. The person being attacked usually isn't capable of resisting the bear so it is up to the rest of the group to distract or deter the bear. This is a volatile situation and everyone is in danger of being injured, but without help the person being dragged off will almost certainly be killed.

Chemical Repellents For Bears

One of the most promising repellents is capsaicin, an ingredient of cayenne peppers. Capsaicin is a powerful local irritant of sensory nerve endings which is widely used as a dog repellent and is commercially available in spray canisters of various sizes (see appendix for sources). Capsaicin products have been tested on captive and free-ranging grizzly and black bears. In the vast majority of the tests, it repelled the bears. The usual behavior pattern for the bears after being sprayed was immediate and vigorous retreat. As of 1989, no aggressive responses to the capsaicin spray have been reported in lab or field tests. But as always with bear behavior, the one thing we know for certain is that we're not certain about much. Behavior varies greatly among individuals, and you may run into a bear that behaves unlike any tested. One thing is for certain; a repellent is to be used only when you or others in your group are in danger. It will be up to the individual to decide the risks and benefits of each situation.

I have chosen to present information on capsaicin because it appears to be the most promising and is what the professionals are carrying in the field. All further references in this section to using a repellent assume that it contains capsaicin and is similar to those listed in the appendix. It's beyond the scope of this book to discuss all the other types of possible repellents, things such as air horns and tear gas. Before considering other types of repellents you should be informed on their testing record and effectiveness. Some so-called repellents may actually increase aggressiveness in bears, which, as you might guess, is the last thing you want to happen in a bear encounter.

If you do choose to carry a repellent, know its limitations. First, the repellent is no good if its packed away when you need it. It needs to be available instantly. Some people use commercial holsters made for the canisters, others rig a system with velcro patches on their pack for a quick release. The next limitation is the spray device. To be effective the spray must hit the bear in the eye. Most of these devices have a very limited range, even on a calm day. Before you take your repellent into the backcountry you should experiment by doing a couple practice sprays with your own canister. This will help you determine accuracy and range and help you estimate how it will respond in field conditions. If you spray one of these canisters into the wind, even a light wind, it will greatly reduce the range of the spray as well as deliver an incapacitating dose in your eyes, nose and throat. This will be extremely unpleasant; study the manufacturer's recommended first aid procedures ahead of time. Should you get into a bear encounter where you have time to think, always consider how wind direction will effect your spray; and better yet, try to avoid having to use the spray at all.

The main danger of carrying a repellent is that it may instill a false sense of security. While they are proven to work, don't bet your life on them if you don't have to. Even if you choose to carry a repellent, you must continue to use all the precautions to avoid bears. Don't hike into a known bear area with the idea of "flushing out some grizz," armed with a can of repellent for protection. Don't creep closer to a feeding bear for that once in a life time photo just because you've got a can of spray on your hip. You are ultimately responsible for your actions; and deliberately disturbing bears or any wildlife is a violation of the park's federal regulations. A repellent is an option of last defense, to be used only after all your efforts to avoid an encounter have failed.

Now that you're feeling very unsure of entering the backcountry, remember again that the chance of encountering a bear is small, especially after taking the proper precautions. Also, the National Park Service helps to prevent hikers from encountering bears by closing off certain areas of the backcountry when these areas have more than the usual amount of bear activity. But a certain amount of fear, or at least consciously thinking about grizzlies, as you hike or camp is part of the Yellowstone experience. Even with all the rangers, regulations, and permits, this is still a wild place, and your safety may hinge on simply a matter of chance. To some people, all the precautions and assurances aren't enough. The presence of bears and the real, or perceived, danger may make hiking in Yellowstone so nerve wracking that the trip becomes unpleasant. Evaluate your fears before you start your trip. Being afraid of bears is not foolish. Don't go if the thought of bears is going to make you miserable. Hiking the backcountry should be an enjoyable experience, not a terrifying one.

On the other end of the spectrum, there are those people who seek out bears, instead of trying to avoid them. Although observing a bear in the backcountry can be the thrill of a lifetime, encountering a bear is risking not only your life, but also the future of that bear. Grizzly bears, especially, cannot cope with human disturbance. In the wild they are unsure of hikers and usually avoid them whenever possible. But if a grizzly is disturbed often enough by hikers and would-be observers, it may leave a prime feeding area to escape this disturbance. Or, rather than trying to escape the cause of the disturbance, the bear may attack it. With the shortage of remaining grizzly habitat left in the lower 48 states, we can't afford to let Yellowstone's grizzlies lose precious feeding areas due to disturbances we can easily prevent. Limit your disturbance of the bears, and heed closures, for the bear's safety and yours.

Spotted Sandpiper
- *head held low*
- *body tilted forward*
- *tail bobs up and down constantly*

WATER TREATMENT

That cold, clear, fast-moving stream certainly looks refreshing on a hot day. The water has a crispness to it that you just don't get from the kitchen tap back home. Of course this stream may also contain some other things you don't have in the water back home. Giardia protozoans and the Campylobactor bacteria are the two most frequently troublesome organisms found in Yellowstone waters; both can cause mild to extreme intestinal distress. How can you know if they're present in the water about to touch your lips? Not by looking and not by tasting. In fact it's difficult for scientists to detect Giardia, even with advanced instrumentation. So how can you be safe? It's fairly simple; treat all the water you drink.

Before we go any further into treatment techniques, a brief description of Giardiasis and Campylobactor is necessary. Giardia lamblia, the most common human intestinal parasite in the U.S., is a pear shaped protozoan that, when ingested in food or drink, may attach itself to our intestinal lining. This changes the absorptive capacity of the intestine and causes the symptoms of Giardiasis. These symptoms appear 1-3 weeks after exposure and may include an explosive onset of watery diarrhea, cramps, gas, abdominal distension, nausea, loss of appetite, vomiting, fever, and chills (Whew!). Acute symptoms usually last an unpleasant 5-7 days. If not treated by medication Giardiasis may go into a chronic stage which is characterized by periodic bouts of less severe symptoms. Check with a physician to see if your case is worth treating with drug therapy. Scientists know that many of the types of animals found in Yellowstone carry a species of Giardia, and that these Giardia may be deposited into water sources through animal feces.

Beaver, for instance, are often accused of passing on Giardia. But whether or not these species of Giardia effect humans has not been proven conclusively, one way or the other.

Campylobactor jejuni, a bacteria, is second only to Giardia as a cause of acute waterborne diarrheal disease. It can be carried in the intestinal tract of humans and many domestic animals, and can be transmitted to humans through water polluted by such carriers. Once in our intestine, the bacteria causes patchy destruction of the mucus lining which in turn may cause bloody diarrhea, abdominal pain, cramps, and fever. These symptoms appear 3-5 days after ingestion and cease within 48-72 hours. The illness is self-limiting and drug therapy is not essential in most cases. If you're out of the backcountry when the illness strikes, it's still worth visiting a physician to play it safe.

After hearing the unattractive details of these illnesses, you're probably more interested in learning how to treat your water. Disinfecting water for drinking can be done a number of ways: filtration, boiling, treating with halogens, and treating with iodine. Treating with halogen or iodine, while effective, involves many variables and won't be discussed here. (See Appendix for references on water treatment). Filter systems are easily obtained and available in a variety of sizes and prices, but manufacturer's directions must be followed. The maximum effective filter pore size for Giardia is 5 microns; for enteric bacteria (such as Campylobactor) it is 0.2 microns. Pre filtering may be necessary for cloudy water and the filter elements have to be replaced or cleaned periodically according to the manufacturer's recommendations.

Possibly the simplest way to treat water in Yellowstone is to bring it to a boil. In the past, numerous publications have recommended treating water by boiling it anywhere from 1 to 30 minutes, depending on the altitude. It appears now that this was overkill. Giardia is very heat sensitive, killed within 5 minutes at 131 degrees F and more rapidly at higher temperatures. Bacteria are slightly more heat resistant but will be killed, along with the Giardia, by any water brought to a boil as disinfection is occurring during the time required to heat water from 140 degrees to boiling. Thus the Wilderness Medical Society and the Journal of the American Medical Association have both stated that any water brought to a boil, even at high altitude, should be safe to drink. A convenient way to handle water for long trips is to boil enough drinking water each night for use on the trail the next day. This way the water has a chance to chill down over night so that it's good and cool by the next day.

While there is no disputing that absolute safety from picking up a waterborne illness requires water treatment, there is some skepticism on the part of long-time Yellowstone backcountry users on the likelihood of contracting one of these illnesses from the park's waters. Many of these people have been drinking the water, without any form of purification, for years without apparently getting sick. There are three possible explanations for this. 1) *The number of human-specific Giardia or harmful bacteria in the water these people have been drinking is relatively low and they have just not ingested any Giardia or bacteria.* This is difficult to prove either way. Giardia and Campylobactor concentration levels would be very difficult to determine and could obviously change quite frequently. Because scientists are still unsure of which animals, other than man, transmit human-specific Giardia into water sources, it is impossible to even estimate possible Giardia levels in wilderness lakes and streams. 2) *Long time backcountry users have acquired an immunity to the Giardia and even though they have ingested contaminated water, they show no symptoms of giardiasis.* This is probably the most frequent rationale used by non treatment proponents, as well as the most macho. It is inherently satisfying to claim that you don't need to treat the water because you have such a strong constitution. This claim may have a basis in truth. A number of studies have shown that some people can develop immunity to Giardia, especially after repeated exposure. 3) *They have developed mild cases of giardiasis and not recognized it as such.* This also seems quite possible. Many people infected with Giardia may only show mild to moderate symptoms. These can disappear without treatment after a variable period of time, usually less than 3 months. Bouts such as these are what may lead to relative immunity from Giardia later.

Although I've shown you the down side to waterborne illnesses; I've also shown you possible reasons why some people who don't treat their water may not get severely ill, and why they may continue drinking untreated water without ever getting severely ill. I've done this so that you will have the facts when it comes time for you to decide whether or not to treat your water. Let me make it clear that I recommend treating water, especially for people relatively new to drinking water in the backcountry. You may indeed fit into one of the above three situations; but why chance it? There are cases every summer in Yellowstone of people who contract one of these illnesses; afterwards, they all wish they would have treated their water. Remember, there is a lot we don't know about these internal parasites and their long term affects. If you're lucky enough never to have had one, there's really no need to pick one up now. Not when boiling your water is so simple.

Great Grey Owl

26

River and Stream Crossings

The trails of Yellowstone cross many rivers and streams, most of which are not bridged. So unless you're able to find a fallen log or logs on which to cross, you'll have to wade to get to the other side. Here are some suggestions that should help you in your stumbling through Yellowstone's ice cold streams.

—If many crossings, or one especially wide crossing, are to be included on your hike, wear wading shoes. Many people use old running shoes or river runner sandals. Rocky stream beds can wreak havoc on bare feet and the pain can make it hard to keep you mind on your balance.

—Don't wade a stream with your hiking boots on. Wet shoes not only cause blisters but they also cause cold feet. More than one person has crossed a stream during the day with their boots on, then taken them off at camp that night, and found them frozen rock-hard the next morning. Also, if the crossing is higher than where you can roll up your pants, take them off or wear shorts. I believe it was Plato that once said, "Wet pants are cold pants."

—You don't have to cross a stream exactly at the trail. Many times there is a shallower or easier crossing a short ways up or downstream.

—If a ford is fast and over thigh deep, forget it. Try another spot or look for a log jam. One slip in that depth of fast water with a backpack and you could easily drown. If you do cross a deep, fast stream, be certain to unbuckle your pack's waist strap if it is not the quick release variety.

—If you must cross a high, fast stream, a light (5mm or ¼ in. thick) rope about 70 to 100 feet long is a good safety device. It won't keep you from getting wet if you slip, but it will keep you from getting swept away.

—Avoid hazardous stream crossings altogether by picking another trail or waiting for the streams to go down. The trail descriptions in this guide provide information on each stream crossing.

WEATHER

The weather and your ability to deal with it are important factors in the success of your hike. As mothers have been telling us all along, getting too cold and wet, or too hot, is not good for us. And in the backcountry, it can be downright dangerous. The best way to compensate for the weather is to take the proper clothing. Choosing the proper clothing would be much easier if you could go by the weather forecast, but you can't. You might notice that when you ask a ranger what the day's weather will be, he or she will hesitate, then while looking very uncomfortable, will mutter something about "partly cloudy, chance of rain." This is the sign of an experienced ranger because they know that on any given summer day in Yellowstone the weather can be hot and sunny one minute, sprinkling rain the next, and turning to windy hail and even snow the next. This means that the well prepared hiker must be ready for the extremes no matter how pleasant the weather appears at the start of the hike (see section on equipment).

Most of Yellowstone's trails are at an elevation of 7,000-9,000 feet above sea level, so that when it gets cloudy, it gets cool. And when it rains, it's a cold rain. Getting cold and wet can easily lead to hypothermia, a lowering of the body's temperature which can sometimes cause death. Thus, it's important that you always carry some protection against cold and rain while hiking at this high elevation. There is a very informative brochure on hypothermia available at any Visitor Center or Ranger Station. For the majority of hikers in Yellowstone, hypothermia is one of the biggest dangers you'll face. It's well worth your time to know how to prevent and treat it.

It's not always cold and wet in Yellowstone, in fact, most summer days are sunny and dry. As nice as this weather feels, there are some things for which to beware. At Yellowstone's high elevation the effects of the sun are magnified. It's quite easy to get a first rate sunburn in no time at all. Protect your eyes with good sunglasses and your skin with sunscreen, especially if travelling over snow. Yellowstone has a very low humidity. Perspiration evaporates rapidly, which means you may not need as much deodorant as usual but you will need more water. For a full day hike most people need 4 or more quarts of water. Unfortunately even when it's available to them, few people will actually drink that much water on a hike. As a result dehydration may limit their performance and energy level. Force yourself to drink, even when you're not thirsty. On hot days, don't drink too much at once, instead drink a little and drink often. Luckily, almost every trail in Yellowstone has an abundance of water nearby (see Water Treatment section), and those that don't are mentioned in the trail descriptions.

WHAT TO EXPECT FROM THE WEATHER:

Mid May-mid June: Temperatures on clear nights 10-30 degrees F.; on sunny days 45-65 degrees F. Rain is common, but it can snow heavily at any time. Snow is still on the ground in the forests and at high elevations. Trails are wet and mucky. Streams are rising. Flowers are blooming at lower elevations. Insects not yet a problem. Migratory birds arrive. Migratory mammals at low elevations but beginning to move to summer range.

Mid June-mid July: Temperatures on clear nights 15-40 degrees F.; on sunny days 55-75 degrees F. Weather improves in July. Meadows may still be wet and mucky; trails are wet but may dry by the end of this period. Streams are at their highest. Mosquitoes are reaching their peak. Flowers blooming over most of the park. Migratory mammals have moved to their summer range.

Late July-mid-August: Temperatures on clear nights 25-40 degrees F.; on sunny days 60-75 degrees F. Most days are sunny with an occasional afternoon rain. Mosquitoes are declining. Trails are dry. Streams are receding. Flowers blooming at higher elevations. Migratory mammals on high ridges and meadows. Berries are ripe on bushes.

Late August-late September: Temperatures on clear nights 15-35 degrees F.; late September: on sunny days 40-55 degrees F. When the weather is fair and sunny, the hiking at this time of year is very enjoyable. Heavy snow falls are possible during this month so be certain to carry the proper cold weather gear. The large animals are congregating at the lower elevations and this is an excellent time to view them. Streams are down. Hunting season opens outside the park in some areas; wear bright clothing if hiking near the boundary.

October: Temperatures on clear nights 0-35 degrees F.; on sunny days 40-55 degrees F. When the weather is fair and sunny, the hiking at this time of year is very enjoyable. Heavy snow falls are common during this month so be certain to carry the proper cold weather gear. The animals are congregating at the lower elevations and this is an excellent time to view them. Streams are down.

THINGS OF INTEREST IN THE BACKCOUNTRY

Hiking is usually more enjoyable when you understand or know something about the things you're seeing along the trail. Guidebooks on flowers, trees, mammals and birds are helpful in this respect and are available from Yellowstone's Visitor Centers. National Park Service naturalist-led walks into the backcountry are another aid. Knowledge gained on one of these walks can often be applied on your own hikes along other trails in the park. The following section of this guide presents information on some of the interesting features found in the backcountry, and provides just a hint of the huge body of knowledge that awaits those interested hikers. Be careful though, a little knowledge can be a dangerous thing; learning about Yellowstone can turn into a life-long addiction.

HYDROTHERMAL AREAS (HOT SPRINGS AND GEYSERS)

A hydrothermal area is a place where water that has been heated by a deep chamber of molten rock comes to the surface in the form of geysers, hot springs, mud pots or fumaroles. There are other hydrothermal areas in the world, but Yellowstone contains more geysers than the rest of these areas combined. The most impressive examples of Yellowstone's hydrothermal features are found in the Upper, Midway, and Lower Geyser Basins along the Firehole River, and also at Norris Geyser Basin. These areas are all accessible by short asphalt and wood walkways. Inexpensive trail leaflets and N.P.S. guided walks both provide interesting geologic background on the workings of these areas' unique features. Thus, if you're interested in hydrothermal features you may want to visit these non-backcountry sites first so that you'll understand more about what you're seeing when you do visit the backcountry hot springs. Two of the larger backcountry hydrothermal areas are the Shoshone Geyser Basin and the Heart Lake Geyser Basin, both of which contain active geysers. Some other interesting backcountry sites include Ponuntpa Springs and the Mudkettles in the Pelican Valley Area, Imperial and Lone Star Geysers in the Firehole Area, Highland Hot Springs on the Mary Mountain Trail, and Washburn Hot Springs on the Washburn Spur Trail. There are many other smaller thermal areas scattered throughout the backcountry which may or may not be found on maps. Part of the intrigue of hiking in Yellowstone is unexpectedly finding one of these areas on your own. Remember: bathing, washing dishes, or cooking is not allowed in thermal features or their runoff channels. The preservation of the delicate mineral formations and the fragile ecosystems living here is a bigger priority than a hot bath.

FOREST FIRE AREAS

The forest fires of 1988 had a major impact on Yellowstone's backcountry. Approximately 800,000 acres in the park burned. For hiking purposes, the Lamar Area and the Snake River Area probably received the greatest impacts from the fires. Still, many trails in the park were not touched. And even those that were burned, did so to varying degrees. Burning varied from places where entire trees were completely burned, to places where only the understory burned and the forest canopy was untouched. This has left us with patterns of different intensities of burns throughout the forest. These patterns are called fire "mosaics" and are especially visible from overlooks and high peaks (such as Mt. Washburn and Mt. Sheridan) Many books have been written about the chronology of events, the policies of management, the fire fighting effort and the effects of those incredible fires (see appendix). I will only touch on the subject briefly here; although it deserves a deeper understanding from anyone interested in Yellowstone's ecology and management.

Forest fires are as much a part of Yellowstone's ecology as are the grizzly bears, the ospreys or the pine trees. For thousands of years lightning has started fires here, and nature has eventually put them out. Fires usually burn themselves out when they come to a stream or river, a wet meadow, a different type or age of tree, or when a rainstorm or snowfall extinguishes them. The number of fires and the extent of the burning depends largely on the weather and the age of the forest. The extremely dry weather and the incredible winds are what drove the huge fires of the summer of 1988. And just as it has for thousands of years, nature finally put the fires out. These burned areas, from recent as well as from past fires, offer the backcountry traveler a first hand look at the natural succession of forests.

When a fire strikes a forest it may burn away the forest canopy. This allows more sunlight to reach the forest floor, and soon grasses, flowers, bushes, and new trees spring up. It's been found that the number of plant species increases after a fire and reaches a peak after about 25 years. Then as the trees grow back up and the forest canopy again forms, the plant diversity decreases drastically. As you'll notice, there isn't much variety to the plant life in a typical lodgepole pine forest.

The number of mammals and birds also increases after a fire. Grazing animals, especially moose, and root eating rodents are attracted by the sudden abundance of ground plants. Some birds nest in the trees killed by the fires while others come to feed on the insects these trees attract. As the forest grows back and its diversity decreases, the diversity and number of birds, rodents and grazing animals also decreases.

After a summer of hiking through these burned areas I noticed some good things and some bad things from a hiker's point of view. The bad is mainly the soot and the heat. The lack of a forest canopy lets the sun glare down and the black trees seem to absorb the heat; and some of these burned areas go on for miles. It all makes for hot hiking. Even sitting down for a rest leaves your clothes and pack streaked in black. Also beware of taking shelter amongst burned trees during windstorms. Some of these trees were burned almost completely through at their bases, and they may need only a small amount of wind from the right direction to be blown down. On the plus side of the fires is the new undergrowth, with large

31

patches of purple fireweed, yellow arnica, and green grass that seem so much brighter when contrasted with the black background. And of course I saw more elk and deer and moose, either because they were in the burned areas to feed or else I could just see further due to the lack of foliage. With the forest canopy gone there are now new views of surrounding peaks where before all you could see were the trees a few yards in front of you. Even the burned trees themselves present images of interesting patterns and forms, which may or may not take your mind off the soot and the heat. Will the scorched earth ruin your hike? All I can say for sure is that the burned areas are worth taking a look at. You may hate them or you may find them fascinating, but you shouldn't miss the opportunity to see them for yourself.

FOSSIL FORESTS

Yellowstone has the most extensive fossil forests of any known area in the world. The park's fossil forests contain many petrified trees standing upright in the position which they originally grew thousands, and even millions of years ago. In a cliff on Specimen Ridge there stands 27 different layers of petrified trees exposed in a vertical succession. These trees became petrified when they were saturated with volcanic outpourings from Yellowstone's numerous past volcanic eruptions. This silica-rich volcanic material filled the cell cavities of the trees, thus preserving their structure for us to view and study today. The petrified trees are mainly sycamores, walnuts, magnolias, chestnuts, oaks, redwoods, maples and dogwoods, which show that Yellowstone must once have had a much warmer climate. The best place to view the standing petrified trees is near the Specimen Ridge Trail. Pieces of petrified wood may also be found along many of the trails in the eastern section of the park, near the volcanic Absaroka Range, Collecting specimens is a violation of park regulations. Leave it for others to discover as you did.

Petrified trees near Crystal Creek.

BACKCOUNTRY WATERFALLS

Trying to describe the individual beauties of Yellowstone's different backcountry waterfalls would be hard for most writers and a definite mistake for this one. Let me just present you with a list of some of the park's highest backcountry falls and leave the rest to your imagination. None of them are ugly and they are all a worthwhile destination.

—Union Falls, Ouzel Falls, Silver Scarf Falls, Dunanda Falls, and Colonnade Falls, along with many others, in the Bechler Area.
—Fairy Falls and Mystic Falls in the Firehole Area.
—Osprey Falls, Wraith Falls, and Knowles Falls in the Mammoth Area.

WILDLIFE

The opportunity to view wildlife is one of the main reasons people venture into Yellowstone's backcountry. Watching an animal act and react in its natural surroundings, away from the crowds, can be a very satisfying experience. Thus perhaps the most interesting thing about Yellowstone's wildlife is that they are all on their own. Finding all their own food, protecting themselves from predators, raising their young, and surviving long cold winters are all part of an animal's life here. As happens in any natural area, some die each year due to winter, predators, old age, disease or a combination of these factors. But their death makes room for other animals and their bodies return to the soil or provide food for scavengers. This is how the animals have lived for centuries in Yellowstone, and we as hikers are privileged to be able to watch as this cycle continues. The following segment contains general information on some of the animals in which people seem most interested.

Grizzly Bear

Grizzly bears represent different things to different people. To some the grizzly is an indicator of the wildness of a place; if a piece of land has grizzlies, than it still must be somewhat untamed and uncivilized. To others the bear is an intelligent animal, with human-like attributes, that just wants to live out its life and be left alone. And to many, the grizzly bear is a powerful predator, to be respected and feared. What is particularly fascinating about grizzlies is how hard their behavior is to predict. The bear's behavior and habits always seem to be one step ahead of the people that think they know the bear the best. Just when researchers, rangers, park management, local residents, photographers, or hikers think they know what a grizzly will do or how it will react in a certain situation, it does something different. It may be that we are poor observers and have a hard time "thinking like a bear", or it may be that the bear's behavior is constantly evolving in response to a changing environment. Which ever it may be, the grizzly is truly an unknown quantity- a wild card; and in our orderly society, we seem to find this particularly intriguing.

When the grizzlies emerge from their den between March and April, Yellowstone is still covered with deep snow. The bear feeds on the carcasses of winter killed animals during this time and can be very protective of the carrion, often times burying it, as well as chasing off hungry ravens and coyotes. When the elk begin calving in May, grizzlies start preying on the elk calves, searching them out where they hide or chasing them down. During late May and June, the cutthroat trout begin moving out of Yellowstone Lake and up into tributary streams to spawn. Bears easily scoop out the trout that are bunched in these streams and can end up eating quite a few pounds of fish each day. As new vegetation begins to emerge and mature, grizzlies also turn to plants, such as grasses and clover, for a part of their diet.

Later on in mid summer the bears graze on clover, dandelion, elk thistle, and the roots of yampa and biscuitroot. The bear's dexterity in digging out the yampa roots is impressive, as the root is small and the plant very delicate. Throughout the summer, grizzlies may prey on an occasional elk as well as dig up pocket gophers. If you see a grizzly intensely digging out in a meadow with periodic lunges and flurries of activity, the quarry is probably a pocket gopher. These tiny animals must be quite a delicacy to the grizzly, as a bear seems to move a lot of earth just to get a gopher in its mouth. Later on, in August and early September, the bears also feed on grouse whortleberry and huckleberries.

During the fall, most grizzlies spend their time in the higher elevations searching out caches of whitebark pine nuts that red squirrels have gathered for the winter. The grizzlies depend on the squirrels to do the meticulous work of gathering the cones and storing them in underground caches; then the bears come in and ransack the caches while all the squirrel can do is chatter in frustration from a nearby tree. The nuts are a very important food source as they provide the fat the bears need to last through a long winter. In years of poor pine nut production, bears must find another fall food source; and this is when they may seek out human foods and move into developed areas or check out backcountry campsites. There are other food sources available to bears in the fall, and some bears do prey on elk, but I'm sure it's a lot easier raiding a squirrel's nut cache than it is chasing down an elk.

When winter arrives the grizzlies den up in one sort of a natural shelter or another, a log pile or a cave for instance. Or else they may dig their own den under the roots of a tree. It's been theorized that grizzlies may wait until a heavy falling snow before they move into their den. This snow covers their tracks and covers their den, insulating them and helping to assure them of an undisturbed winter slumber.

Elk

Of Yellowstone's large mammals, the elk is the most abundant and thus most often spotted in the backcountry. Most elk spend the summers near high meadows where they feed on grasses, sedges and forbs. Big Game Ridge, Two Ocean Plateau, the Gallatin Range, and the upper Miller Creek and upper Lamar River areas are all excellent spots to view elk during the summer. In the fall the elk move to lower elevations for the mating season. The bulls perform their famous antler to antler battles and sound their challenging bugles as they strive to acquire, and horde, a harem of females. Some of the best fall viewing spots for elk are Swan Lake Flats, Gallatin River Valley, Slough Creek, Big Game Ridge and Two Ocean Plateau.

Bison

Yellowstone's bison are actually hybrid descendants of the plains bison and the mountain bison. Mountain bison originally inhabited Yellowstone but were hunted to near extinction by the late 1800's. Plains bison were then brought into the park to supplement the population and the two species interbred. The present bison population though, has taken after the mountain bison in their migrating habits and behavior. Unlike the huge herds that used to roam the plains, Yellowstone's bison generally travel in small bands of 10-40 animals, consisting of cows, young bulls, calves and occasional mature bulls. (The bison may gather in larger herds during the rut, from mid July to mid August, and on wintering grounds. These herds may contain as many as 450 animals). Many of the bull bison travel in their own small groups of 3-8; and often when a bull gets on in age, it no longer travels with the herd and may be seen feeding by itself miles from any other bison. Like the elk, the bison spend the winters at lower elevations such as the lower Yellowstone River area, Firehole Valley, and Lamar Valley. Many bison winter in Pelican Valley and Hayden Valley, which at almost 8,000 feet aren't low, but they are filled with lush vegetation for grazing. To reach this vegetation requires pushing aside a lot of snow with the bison's head and hooves. In the early summer the bison move surprisingly fast to high meadows where they graze until September. Here their mountain bison blood really comes through as they wander above the tree line and scamper along rocky ledges that seem more appropriate for bighorn sheep. Places where you might spot bison during the summer include Little Firehole Meadows, Pitchstone Plateau, Canoe Lake area, Specimen Ridge, and Hayden Valley.

In recent years bull bison have butted or gored about two dozen people, often resulting in injury or death. While most bison in the backcountry will run from you, some old bulls will seem to be oblivious to your presence. They aren't. And they can move very fast when they want to. Do not approach closer than a hundred yards to any bison. Detour around them, off the trail, if you must.

Other Animals

Coyotes are often spotted in large open meadows such as Hayden Valley, Pelican Valley and Gardners Hole. They spend the summers in these meadows searching for mice and pocket gophers. These rodents are their main food during summer, but in winter the coyotes feed heavily on the carcasses of elk and bison.

Black bears may turn up just about anywhere in Yellowstone, although you probably won't see them begging for food along the roadside as in years past. Black bears seem to prefer forested areas more than large open valleys, and are a fairly secretive creature in the wild. While black bears have been responsible for very few backcountry injuries to hikers, they should still be treated as potentially dangerous, and avoided, especially sows with cubs.

With one exception, bighorn sheep are seldom seen along the park's trails. The sheep spend the warm months on high inaccessible ridges grazing on the alpine plants and getting their water from the snow. Mt. Washburn is the one trail where the chance of spotting bighorn is fairly good.

Moose are frequently seen along the park's trails especially near lakes, ponds and willow lined streams where they feed on aquatic vegetation. The upper Yellowstone River, lower Pelican Valley, Bechler Meadows, Gallatin River, Gardners Hole and the Madison Valley are some of the better places to look for moose.

Yellowstone has over 220 species of birds that live within, or migrate through, its boundaries. Trumpeter swans, osprey, white pelicans, bald eagles, golden eagles and sandhill cranes are a few of the more spectacular. One thing these species have in common is the need to nest away from disturbance. So if on one of your hikes you should spot one of these magnificent birds nesting, observe them from a distance and leave if they appear distressed with your presence.

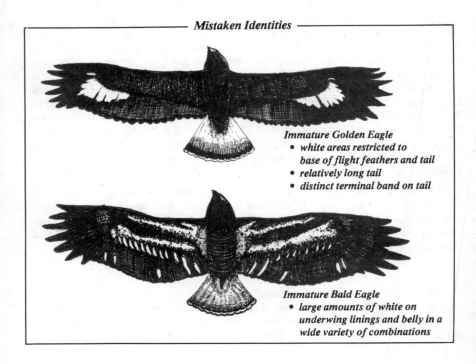

Mistaken Identities

Immature Golden Eagle
- *white areas restricted to base of flight feathers and tail*
- *relatively long tail*
- *distinct terminal band on tail*

Immature Bald Eagle
- *large amounts of white on underwing linings and belly in a wide variety of combinations*

Shooting Star
- *violet flowers*
- *blooms May through August*
- *early spring food for elk*

MAPS

The maps included in this book should be sufficient for planning hikes and navigating on maintained trails in Yellowstone National Park. Even so, larger scale maps are often useful in identifying landmarks and mountain peaks and for finding your exact location along a trail. For off trail hiking, an additional topographic map is often a necessity. The U.S. Geologic Survey has produced two different series of maps for Yellowstone. In the 1950's, the U.S.G.S. mapped the park in the 15 minute series. One inch on these maps equals one mile on the ground. These maps are the perfect size for navigating on or off trail, and as of 1990 are still sold in a number of locations around the park (see appendix for names of local shops and for ordering information). Unfortunately some of the trails shown on these maps are no longer there, or not maintained, or have been rerouted. The same is true of some of the roads. Forest cover patterns may also have changed.

The U.S.G.S. is replacing the 15 minute series with the new larger scale 7½ minute series. It takes 4 of the 7½ minute maps to cover one 15 minute map. The detail is great but you may need to hire a llama just to carry all the maps. These 7½ minute maps will become available to the general public during the early 1990's.

The topographic maps reproduced in this guide are a combination of the 7½ minute maps, 15 minute maps and a 1:125000 scale specialty map of Yellowstone Park. In some cases these maps have been reduced from their original size due to space constraints of the book, but a mileage scale has still been provided for each. Trails that are highlighted and identified on the maps are those that are described in the book. Other trails visible on the maps may be currently maintained trails that were not included due to space constraints as well as the trail's relatively low priority for recreational hikers. Some of these unidentified trails are simply old trails that are in various stages of disuse or regrowth. Check at a local ranger station for current conditions on any of these trails.

TRAIL DESCRIPTIONS

The trail descriptions in the Yellowstone Trail Guide can be used to help you decide what trail to take, when to take that trail, and how hard the hiking will be.

The trail descriptions are divided into 16 different geographical areas. Each area has an introduction which gives general information about that area and its trails. Each trail in the area is then described, usually starting with general information about the trail conditions, scenery along the way, opportunities to see wildlife, and anything else that may help you decide if that's the trail for you. Following this information is a listing of distances, in miles and kilometers, from the trailhead to points along the trail. (1 mile equals 1.6 kilometer). Hiking distances in the guide are not always exact, but are accurate to within a half mile. After the distances comes the more detailed information which, when used in conjunction with the maps included in this guide, will help you in the actual navigation along the trail.

The descriptions in the guide do cover a variety of trail conditions and for each of these conditions certain variables should be taken into consideration. For instance the depth of most stream crossings are given, but these of course will vary with how well you choose a spot to cross and if there has been much recent rainfall. Mosquito concentrations and the degree to which they annoy hikers is a rather subjective matter and can be altered by such variables as cold weather, welcome breezes, and the hiker's own mental state. The maps do not show backcountry campsite locations as they may change from year to year. A campsite map is available by mail from the National Park Service (see appendix for address) or a large scale map can be viewed at any ranger station. Because of the numerous mountain streams in Yellowstone's backcountry, the availability of drinking water is not usually a problem and will only be mentioned if there is a shortage and a need to bring extra water with you.

Throughout this guide you will notice that certain trails have this logo:

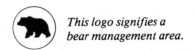 *This logo signifies a
bear management area.*

These trails travel through areas that have scheduled closures or restrictions on their use during certain times of the year. This is an attempt by the National Park Service to allow bears undisturbed use of prime habitat. A list and map of the scheduled closures is available by mail from the National Park Service, Box 168, Yellowstone N.P., WY 82190, or at any ranger station.

NORTHWEST CORNER

The Northwest Corner of Yellowstone is a place of ups and downs. High, steep ridges and low valleys mean long climbs and descents for hikers. There is not much level walking done here. Once atop the rugged heights, the view of the forested hills, mountain peaks, streams, and lakes below is simply inspiring. Chances are good of seeing wildlife anytime of the year in this area. Elk and deer live on the high ridges in the summer and along the river valleys in the spring and fall. Moose are abundant along the willow-lined streams and bighorn sheep inhabit the steep slopes and mountain ridges near Sheep Mtn. and Bighorn Peak. All the trails in this area start from trailheads on U.S. Highway 191, which runs between Bozeman and West Yellowstone, Montana. *Map 1*

DALEY (or DAILY) CREEK TRAIL

From Daley Creek Trailhead (milepost 31 Highway 191) to:

Jct. with Black Butte Trail cutoff	2 miles	3 km
Jct. with Tepee Ck. Trail cutoff	3	5
Jct. with Skyline Trail (Dailey Pass)	5.5	9

The Daley Creek Trail provides the easiest access from Highway 191 to the Skyline Trail. The Daley Creek Trail climbs about 1,600 feet in 5 miles as it follows Daley Creek through meadows and along open hillsides. There are good opportunities to spot moose during the summer, and elk during spring and fall.

After 2 miles, The Daley Creek Trail meets the Black Butte Trail cutoff. (The cutoff turns east. Look for the first trail marker in a clump of trees up the drainage to the east. The cutoff travels approximately 2 miles over a ridge to meet the Black Butte Trail). Further on the Daley Creek Trail, you will meet the Tepee Creek cutoff. (This cutoff travels up through meadows, for approximately 1 mile, to the park boundary and the Tepee Creek Trail in the Gallatin N.F.).

The Daley Creek Trail ends at Dailey Pass on the park's north boundary. From the pass, the Skyline Trail follows the boundary to the east; other trails lead north and west into Gallatin N.F.

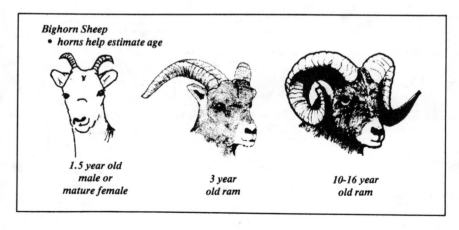

Bighorn Sheep
• *horns help estimate age*

1.5 year old male or mature female

3 year old ram

10-16 year old ram

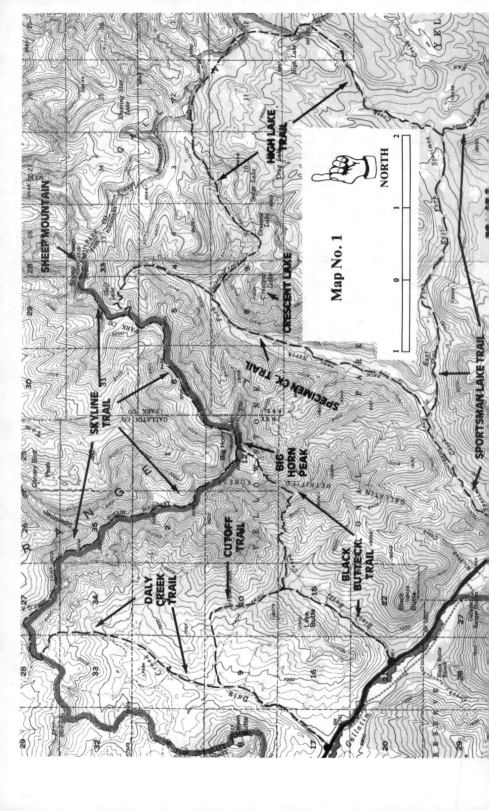

Map No. 1

NORTH

SKYLINE TRAIL

The Skyline Trail provides the best prolonged dose of mountain scenery in Yellowstone. As it follows the boundary ridge of the park the trail offers exciting views of mountain ranges in all directions, as well as travelling to the summit of two mountains itself. Be certain to bring plenty of water on this hike because the only source of water is melting snow, which may be gone by mid August. Several sections of this trail are steep and rocky. Watch your footing. Chances of seeing wildlife along this route are very good. Elk and bighorn sheep feed in high meadows visible from the trail. Ravens, hawks and eagles may be spotted soaring above or even below you. Marmots and pikas scurry among the rocks near the trail. *Map 1*

From junction of Daley Creek Trail with
Skyline Trail to:

Bighorn Peak	6 miles	9.5 km
Jct. with Specimen Creek Trail	9	14.5
Sheep Mountain	10.5	17

Starting from the end of the Daley Creek Trail, at Daley Pass, the Skyline Trail begins climbing up the boundary ridge. The ridge consists of a series of small summits that must be ascended then descended. There are good views of the Gallatin Range and Ramshorn Peak to the north. After a final steep climb of 600 feet, the summit of Bighorn Peak is reached. The junction with the Black Butte Creek Trail is located here. From the summit the Skyline Trail descends and traverses three more small summits to the junction with the Specimen Creek Trail. (The Specimen Creek Trail travels 1/2 mile down to Shelf Lake and then 8 more miles out to Highway 191). From the junction, the Skyline Trail continues steeply up Sheep Mountain, climbing about 1,000 feet in one mile to the summit. When you first see the summit of Sheep Mtn. you may wonder why a drive-in movie screen is sitting on top. Don't wait around for the show because that large object is actually a piece of radio relaying equipment. Look instead for the bighorn sheep that are occasionally spotted in this area.

BLACK BUTTE CREEK TRAIL

From Black Butte Creek Trailhead (milepost 28,
Highway 191) to:

Daley Creek cutoff	2 miles	3 km
Summit of Bighorn Peak	7	11

The Black Butte Creek trail travels from the Gallatin Highway to the Skyline Trail and provides the shortest, as well as steepest, route to the summit of Bighorn Peak. There is a spectacular view in all directions from the top of the trail. The trail climbs 3,100 feet in 7 miles as it follows the forested valley of Black Butte Creek and winds past the Gallatin Petrified Forest. Exposed pieces of petrified wood are common throughout this area. Also watch for moose and mule deer low on the trail, and bighorn sheep higher up. From the summit of Bighorn Peak, it is about 3.5 miles to Shelf Lake following the Skyline Trail east. *Map 1*

SPECIMEN CREEK TRAIL

The Specimen Creek Trail travels from the Gallatin Highway (U.S. 191) to Shelf Lake and the junction with the Skyline Trail on the park's north boundary. The Specimen Creek Trail offers good opportunities to see wildlife. Elk are gathered in this valley from October to June, Moose may be seen anytime along the creek and bighorn sheep frequent the slopes of Meldrum Mountain. *Map 1*

From Specimen Creek Trailhead (milepost 26, Highway 191) to:

Jct. with Sportsman Lake Trail	2 miles	3 km
Jct. with Crescent Lake/ High Lake Tr.	6	9.5
Shelf Lake	8	13
Jct. with Skyline Trail	8.5	14

For the first 6 miles the Specimen Creek Trail climbs slowly through the forest and meadows along Specimen Creek and its North Fork. There are two bridged crossings of the North Fork. At the junction with the Crescent Lake Trail the grade increases; and by the time you reach Shelf Lake two miles away, you will have climbed 1,100 feet. With Sheep Mountain looming above, Shelf Lake is a pleasant spot to rest, enjoy the scenery, and refill your water bottles. It's now about a 1/2 mile hike up to the boundary ridge and the Skyline Trail. The view from the boundary is well worth this extra effort.

CRESCENT LAKE/HIGH LAKE TRAIL

This trail travels from the Specimen Creek Trail to the Sportsman Lake Trail. It offers the opportunity for a superb 22 mile loop hike which takes you past two lovely alpine lakes and over an abundance of rugged mountain country. Although the country seems rugged, the environment of the alpine lakes is fragile. Plants grow slowly and soil is thin and a long time in forming. Treat these places gently. Bring stoves, as fires are prohibited; and be certain to pack out all trash, even if it isn't yours. *Map 1*

From Specimen Creek Trail (6 miles from Specimen Ck. Trailhead) to:

Crescent Lake	1.5 miles	2.2 km
High Lake	6	9.5
Jct. with Sportsman Lake Tr.	9.5	15
Specimen Creek Trailhead via		
Sportsman Lake Trail	16	25.5

The Crescent Lake/High Lake Trail starts from the Specimen Creek Trail, 6 miles in from the trailhead on Highway 191. The first 1.5 mile to Crescent Lake climbs 900 feet up the side of a forested valley. The lake sits in a cirque with an 800 foot cliff rising above it. The trail from Crescent Lake to High Lake is relatively new and may not be on topographic maps put out before 1985. From Crescent Lake the trail travels northeast, climbing up the side of a forested valley. The trail climbs out of that valley and follows the north boundary ridge of the park about 2 miles. There are several steep rocky sections along here. From that ridge the trail veers south downhill, following a little open valley to High lake. High Lake is a beautiful, secluded spot and the feeling of serenity and accomplishment that comes from sitting along its shore is well worth the toil of the hike. From the lake, the Crescent Lake/High Lake Trail continues down the East Fork of Specimen Creek, dropping about 700 feet in the 3 miles before it joins the Sportsman Lake Trail From this junction it's 6 miles back to the Specimen Creek Trailhead on highway 191.

SPORTSMAN LAKE TRAIL—WEST

The Sportsman Lake Trail travels 24 miles from Highway 191 to the Mammoth-Norris Road. It follows the East Fork of Specimen Creek, passes by Sportsman Lake, crosses the Gallatin Range, and ends in Gardners Hole. This segment of the guide will describe the trail from its starting point on Highway 191 to Sportsman Lake. The trail east of that will be covered in the Gallatin section under Sportsman Lake Trail—East. *Maps 1, 2*

From Specimen Creek Trailhead (milepost 26, Highway 191) to:

Jct. with Sportsman Lake Trail	2 miles	3 km
Jct. with High Lake Trail	6.5	10.5
Sportsman Lake	11	17.5
Electric Divide	14	22.4
Glen Creek Trailhead, Mammoth-Norris Road	24	38.5

Starting from the Specimen Creek Trailhead, you actually follow the Specimen Creek trail for the first 2 miles. The meadows in this area are home for moose all year round; and elk gather here from late September through May. After crossing the footbridge over Specimen Creek, the Sportsman Lake Trail follows the East Fork through forest and an occasional meadow. There are two more bridged crossings of the East Fork in this section. The trail then veers away from the East Fork and meets the High Lake Trail. (It's 3.5 miles to High Lake from this junction). The Sportsman Lake Trail continues east, climbing gradually up to a low pass and then dropping down (500 feet in a mile) through burned forest to Sportsman Lake. The lake sits in a meadow at the base of a thousand foot cliff. Moose and elk are occasionally seen feeding in these meadows during the evening. Sportsman Lake is inhabited by cutthroat trout and numerous ducks and coots.

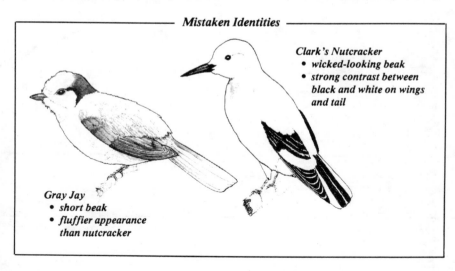

Mistaken Identities

Clark's Nutcracker
- *wicked-looking beak*
- *strong contrast between black and white on wings and tail*

Gray Jay
- *short beak*
- *fluffier appearance than nutcracker*

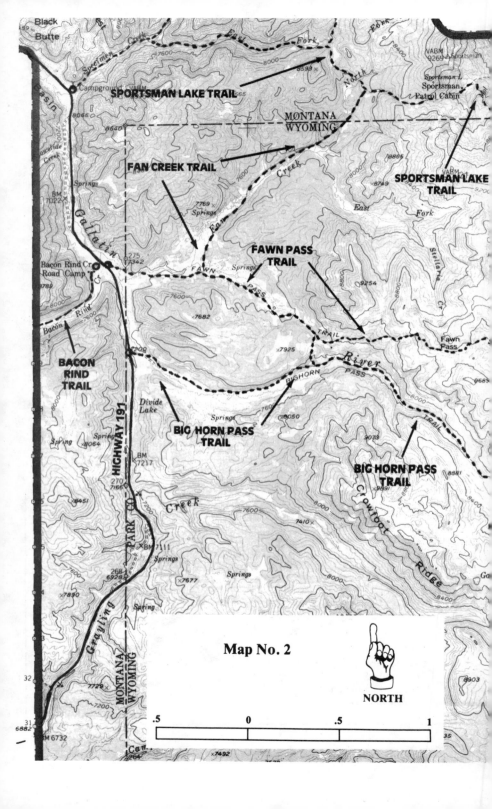

Map No. 2

NORTH

.5   0   .5   1

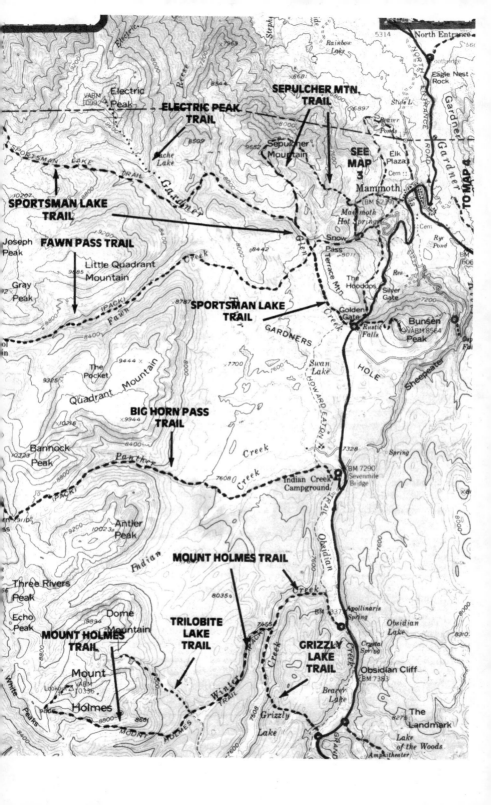

GALLATIN MOUNTAINS AND
THE MAMMOTH AREA

The Gallatin Mountain Range runs south-north from Mt. Holmes to the north border of Yellowstone at Electric Peak . The range continues up into Montana as far north as Bozeman. This guide will deal just with the area inside the boundaries of the park. The Gallatin Area trails start either from the Mammoth-Norris Road or from U.S. Highway 191 (which runs from Bozeman to West Yellowstone Montana).

In this area, the Gallatins are a range of 10,000' high, somewhat rounded, mainly sedimentary peaks. There is an extensive array of trails in this area for those wishing to journey to the higher places of Yellowstone. The Fawn Pass, Bighorn Pass, Mt. Holmes, and Electric Peak Trails all provide the hiker with a chance to get a good feeling for the alpine environment. Besides being an important part of the park's trail system, the range is also an essential part of Yellowstone's ecosystem. Each spring the mountains' melting snows feed such major rivers as the Madison, Gallatin and Gardner. Each summer the area is the home for many of the park's transient large mammals. The high meadows are an escape from the insects, and a place to feed for elk and sheep. The willow-lined streams attract moose and Quadrant Mountain harbors a herd of bighorn sheep. And each fall the lower slopes of the mountains host the famous rut of the elk.

The Gallatins are also the home of the grizzly and black bear. The grasses and forbs favored by the bears grow in the fertile glacial soil of the Gallatin's ridges and valleys. The upper reaches of the range are dotted with whitebark pine, the seeds of which are an important fall food source for the bears. The numerous mountain meadows away from roads and trails also provide the seclusion that the grizzly needs. Because of the bears, there are restrictions on some of the hiking trails in this area. On some of these trails, parties of 4 or more are recommended for day hiking and 4 or more people may be required for overnight camping. From past experience it appears that a group this size is less likely to surprise or be attacked by a bear. Off trail hiking may also be prohibited in some areas. Check at the Mammoth Visitor Center for current regulations.

GRIZZLY LAKE TRAIL

From Mammoth-Norris Road (1 mile south of Beaver Lake) to:

Grizzly Lake	2 miles	3 km
Jct. with Mt. Holmes Trail	3.5	6
Mt. Holmes Trailhead	6	9.5

Grizzly Lake is a fun hike (when the mosquitoes become unbearable, just keep repeating that to yourself). The trailhead is about a mile south of Beaver Lake on the Mammoth-Norris Road at a small paved pull-out. The trail starts out travelling through a meadow in sight of a spectacular forest fire burn. This hillside burned in 1976; and as usually happens, standing dead trees were left in the fire's wake. These standing trees spent the next 12 years getting drier and drier. So when the fire of 1988 hit this incredibly dry wood it erupted into a severe fire storm, leaving an area that looked as if it had been hit by a small atomic bomb. No standing trees

46

were left this time. This relatively small area received an inordinate amount of attention from photographers that needed fire devastation photos.

From the meadow, the trail climbs 250 ft. through the burned hillside to the top of a ridge. The trail travels through burned forest and along a meadow that attracts elk and provides beautiful displays of wildflowers. Just before the trail starts down the west side of the ridge, there is an impressive view of Mt. Holmes and the Gallatin Range that was greatly improved by the fire of 1988. The trail now drops 300 feet to the shore of Grizzly Lake. The lake is set down in a steep valley, which can keep down the afternoon breezes and hold in the mosquitoes. Straight Creek flows from the north end of the lake and can be crossed on a log jam. The Grizzly Lake Trail continues along the west side of Straight Creek through flowering meadows to Winter Creek. At this point Winter Creek can usually be crossed on fallen logs. Once across Winter Creek, the Mt. Holmes Trail is ¼ mile away and the Mt. Holmes Trailhead about 2.5 miles further. *Map 2*

MT. HOLMES TRAIL (WINTER CREEK TRAIL)

The Mt. Holmes Trail is a good two day, one night hike. The trail follows Winter Creek through thick Engleman Spruce, lodgepole pine and subalpine fir forest up to the open talus slopes of Mt. Holmes. The forest, as well as the higher slopes, may hold patches of snow until early July. A wide assortment of wildlife may be spotted on this trail: black bears, grizzly bears, moose elk, pine martens, and blue grouse. Look for ravens, hawks, rosy finches, pikas, and marmots above tree line. *Map 2*

From Mt. Holmes Trailhead (3.5 miles south of Indian Creek Campground on the Mammoth-Norris Road) to:

Winter Creek Ford	1 miles	1.5 km
Jct. with Grizzly Lake Trail	2.5	4
Jct. with Trilobite Lake Trail	5.5	9
Summit of Mt. Holmes	10	16

The Mt. Holmes Trail starts out following a dirt road. After the road ends, the trail travels to Winter Creek and then turns and follows the creek upstream. The creek may be forded or, with some scouting upstream, may be crossed on fallen logs. The forest along this trail sustained various degrees of burn during the 1988 fires, mainly in the first 7 miles. The trail continues through the forest to the junction with the Grizzly Lake Trail. At this junction the trail climbs up above Winter Creek for the next 3/4 mile. At Winter Creek Meadows you will find a N.P.S. patrol cabin, a campsite, and the junction with the Trilobite Lake Trail. Now the trail climbs steadily through forest and another large open area to the saddle between the White Peaks and Mt. Holmes. From the saddle the trail climbs steeply (1,000 ft. in a mile) up the loose rock to the 10,336 foot summit of Mt. Holmes. The view from the top takes in the Gallatin Range to the north, the Absaroka Range to the east and even the Teton Range to the south. The summit also has a fire lookout that is manned most of the summer.

TRILOBITE LAKE TRAIL

Mount Holmes Trailhead (approximately 3 miles south of Indian Creek Campground on the Mammoth-Norris Road) to:

Grizzly Lake Trail Jct.	2.5 miles	4 km
Trilobite Lake Trail Jct.	5.5	9
Trilobite Lake	8	12

Trilobite Lake is a beautiful little lake set in the cirque of Mt. Holmes, Trilobite Ridge and Dome Mountain. This trip is a good, but long, dayhike or an even better overnight trip. Start at the Mount Holmes Trailhead and follow the Winter Creek/ Mt. Holmes Trail for 5.5 miles to the big meadows of Winter Creek. Here you'll find the closest campsite to Trilobite Lake and the junction with the Trilobite Lake Trail. The Trilobite Lake Trail heads northwest and climbs about 700 vertical feet in the next 2.5 miles. It travels through forest that was burned to varying degrees in the 1988 fire and past a big blowdown from the spring of 1989. There are non-native brook trout in the lake. *Map 2*

BIGHORN PASS TRAIL

The Bighorn Pass Trail crosses the Gallatin Mountain Range as it travels from the Mammoth-Norris Road to the Gallatin Highway. The scenery varies from grass and willow river valleys to dense forest, to high meadows. There is also a variety of wildlife, including grizzlies, to be seen along this trail. Because of the high concentrations of bears in the area there are special restrictions on hiking the Bighorn Pass Trail. Parties of 4 or more people are recommended and may be required for overnight trips. Off-trail travel is not permitted in some areas. Check at Mammoth Visitor Center for current regulations. *Map 2*

From Indian Creek Campground (on Mammoth-Norris Road) to:

Indian Creek footbridge	2 miles	3 km
Panther Creek footbridge	3	5
Bighorn Pass	8	13
Jct. with cutoff trail to Fawn Pass	14.5	23
U.S. Highway 191 (milepost 20.5)	19	30

This trail begins on the west side of the bridge on the Indian Creek Campground entrance road. The trail skirts south around the campground before paralleling Indian Creek for 2 miles through willow meadows and lodgepole pine forest. This is a good area for a short morning or evening hike from the campground, as there are almost always moose or elk feeding in these meadows. After a bridged crossing of Indian Creek the trail climbs a small ridge, then drops down to Panther Creek. The trail crosses Panther Creek by bridge and runs through a pine, spruce and fir forest. At about the 6 mile point the trail will break out of the forest. Look for evidence in this area of a fairly large avalanche that slid off Bannock Peak, north of the trail, in the early spring of 1986. Jumbled piles of trees from the slide litter both sides of the trail. As you near the pass, the trail gets steeper and climbs 1,100 feet in the last 2 miles. As you hike this section, watch the slopes of Bannock Pk. and Quadrant Mountain for bighorn sheep. From the pass, the view west of the Gallatin River Valley may prompt you to just sit back and absorb the scenery the rest of the day.

The trail descends steeply from the pass to the Gallatin River and follows it through forest and meadows to the junction with the cutoff trail to Fawn Pass. This cutoff trail allows you to make a loop-hike-of-sorts between the two trails. The Bighorn Pass Trail continues 4 more miles to the Gallatin River footbridge. The meadows along the river here are excellent spots to view elk from late September through early June. The trail continues a short distance to the trailhead on Highway 191.

FAWN PASS TRAIL

The Fawn Pass Trail crosses the Gallatin Mountain Range as it travels from the Mammoth-Norris Road to the Gallatin Highway (U.S. 191). The scenery varies from grass and willow river valleys to dense forest to mountain meadows. Much of the forested sections of this trail were burned to varying degrees in the fires of 1988. A variety of wildlife, including grizzly bears may be spotted along this trail at any time of the year. Because of the high concentrations of bears in this area, parties of 4 or more people are recommended for day hiking. Parties of 4 of more may be required for overnight trips; and off-trail travel may not be allowed. Check at Mammoth Visitor Center for current regulations before hiking this trail. *Map 2*

From Glen Creek Trailhead to:

Fawn Pass Trail leaves old road	2 miles	3 km
Gardner River footbridge	4	6
2nd crossing of Fawn Creek	5.5	9
Fawn Pass	12	19
Cutoff trail to Bighorn Pass	16	26
Jct. with Fan Creek Trail	19.5	31
Highway 191 (milepost 22)	21	34

The trail starts at the Glen Creek Trailhead, which is about 5 miles south of Mammoth on the Mammoth-Norris Road, directly across from the entrance to the Bunsen Peak Road. The trail is actually an old road for the first two miles. After 2 miles, the Fawn Pass Trail leaves the old road and heads west. (The old road continues to Snow Pass and leads back to the Mammoth area).

The Fawn Pass Trail now starts climbing over a 500 foot high ridge through meadows and stands of aspen. From this ridge there are good views of Gardners Hole and the southern portion of the Gallatin Range. This is also an excellent area for spotting elk during late September and October. The trail drops down the ridge's other side to the Gardner River valley and crosses the river on a double log bridge. A short distance further Fawn Creek is crossed the same way. There is an impressive view of Electric Peak (north) from this area, and moose are often spotted here during the summer. The trail climbs gradually through the forest, following Fawn Creek, and crosses it once more (calf deep crossing after mid July). Soon after the crossing the trail starts climbing moderately, gaining 1,100 feet in the last 5 miles to Fawn pass at 9,100 feet. From the open meadows of the pass there are good views of to the west of the Gallatin River Valley and the Madison Range. Traveling west, the trail descends 1,100 feet in 4 miles down to the cutoff trail to Bighorn Pass. By taking the cutoff trail, a loop-hike-of-sorts can be made of the Fawn Pass and Bighorn Pass trails. The Fawn Pass Trail continues through meadows that hold large numbers of elk from late September through May.

1.5 miles before reaching U.S. 191, the Fawn Pass Trail meets the Fan Creek Trail. By taking the Fan Creek Trail to the Sportsman Lake Trail, then following the Sportsman Lake Trail to the Glen Creek Trailhead, a beautiful 43 mile loop hike may be done.

From the Fan Creek Junction, the Fawn Pass Trail continues to a bridge over Fan Creek and then on to the bridge over the Gallatin River. The trail ends a few hundred yards further at Milepost 22 on Highway 191.

SPORTSMAN LAKE TRAIL—EAST

The eastern section of the Sportsman Lake Trail travels from the Mammoth-Norris Road to Sportsman Lake. Whether you hike just a portion, or all of this section of trail, you'll find the scenery interesting and varied. The trail takes you through the sage and grass of Gardners Hole, past meadows and stands of Douglas fir along Glen Creek, across the clear Gardner River, up and over the rocky meadows of Electric Divide, and finally down through a burned forest to Sportsman Lake.

There is almost always wildlife to be spotted along this trail. Elk and bighorn sheep are seen near Electric Divide during the summer, and moose near Sportsman Lake and in Gardners Hole. Hiking along Glen Creek in the fall is an excellent way to spot elk. Early in the morning during rutting season, the bulls will be out in the meadows bugling, sparring, and just generally putting on a great show. The Sportsman Lake Trail also goes through some prime grizzly bear habitat near Electric Divide, so be certain to take proper precautions. Overnight trips in this area require a party of 4 or more people. The same is recommended for day hikes, but is not required. Off-trail hiking is not allowed in some areas. Check at Mammoth Visitor Center for current regulations. *Map 2*

From Glen Creek Trailhead (5 miles south of Mammoth) to:

Jct. with Fawn Pass Trail	2 miles	3 km
Jct. with Sepulcher Mtn. Trail	3	5
Gardner River	6	9.5
Electric Divide	10	16
Sportsman Lake	14	22.5
Specimen Creek Trailhead	24	38.5

The Sportsman Lake Trail starts at the Glen Creek Trailhead just south of Rustic Falls and directly across from the entrance to the Bunsen Peak Road (on the Mammoth-Norris Road). The first 2 miles of the trail are on an old road through a sage meadow which was burned over in the fires of 1988. After about 2 miles, the trail veers west of this road and on to the junction with the Fawn Pass Trail. (If you had stayed on the old road it would lead you to Snow Pass and down to Mammoth Hot Springs). From the junction with Fawn Pass Trail, the Sportsman Lake Trail continues along Glen Creek where it meets the Sepulcher Mtn. Trail (it's about 2 miles and 2,300 vertical feet to the summit of Sepulcher from here). The Sportsman Trail stays on an open hillside, climbing gradually and paralleling

50

Glen Creek, until it enters the forest and leaves the creek. This brings you to the top of a forested ridge above the Gardner River. Here our trail meets the Electric Peak Spur Trail. From this junction the Sportsman Lake Trail drops down to the Gardner River. You must now cross the Gardner; which is calf deep in late summer and fall, but thigh deep and swift during the early season snow melt. Electric Divide is about 4 miles and 2,000 vertical feet away. After crossing the river, the trail starts climbing, crosses the river again, and continues uphill through forest to Electric Divide.

From the divide, the trail descends steeply 2,100 feet in 3 miles to Sportsman Lake. This area was burned to varying degrees by the fires of 1988. The lake, which contains cutthroat trout sits in a meadow at the base of a thousand foot cliff. Moose and elk are frequently spotted in the meadow during the morning and evening. From the lake, the trail continues west to Highway 191, 10 miles away. This section of the trail is described in the Sportsman Lake Trail-West segment of this book.

HOWARD EATON TRAIL—MAMMOTH TO GOLDEN GATE
(3.5 miles, 5.6 km)

This trail travels through some interesting terrain, including the Mammoth Hot Springs and the Hoodoos, and provides the opportunity for a medium length loop hike from the Mammoth Area. The trail starts at the Clematis Trailhead, in the gulch just north of the Liberty Cap and just south of a grey stone house in Mammoth Village. The Howard Eaton Trail veers left (south) after a couple hundred yards and begins climbing steeply up towards the Upper Terrace Drive. The trail passes some hotsprings, parallels the Upper Terrace Drive, then continues south through limber pine and juniper, as it climbs up away from the hot springs area. About 1.2 miles from the trailhead the Howard Eaton Trail passes the junction with the Snow Pass Trail. It continues climbing up through the Hoodoos, which are a huge, jumbled collection of limestone boulders that have sheared off and tumbled down from the cliffs to the west. The trail eventually tops out on the shoulder of Terrace Mountain, where there is a good view of the Gallatin Range. The trail has climbed about 1,100 vertical feet from the trailhead. The Howard Eaton trail now descends to the Glen Creek Trail (or Sportsman Lake Trail-East) about 300 yards from the Glen Creek Trailhead at Golden Gate. To loop back to Mammoth (3.4 miles) take the Glen Creek Trail northwest to Snow Pass. *Map 3*

BACON RIND CREEK TRAIL
(2 miles, 3 km)

The Bacon Rind Creek Trail starts at a service road at milepost 22.5 on Highway 191. Unlike the other trails in the area, this trail starts on the west side of the highway. This easy trail travels through meadows and forest edge along Bacon Rind Creek to Yellowstone's West Boundary. Willows in the meadows provide food for moose and elk; and grizzly bears roam the area as well. From the park boundary the trail heads up towards the high peaks of the Lee Metcalf Wilderness Area. Check at a U.S.F.S. Ranger Station for information on this trail. *Map 2*

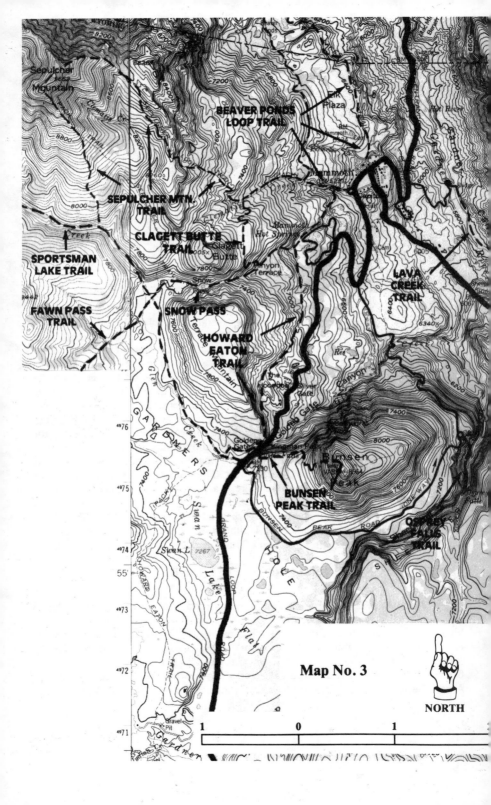

Map No. 3

NORTH

SPORTSMAN LAKE TRAIL

FAWN PASS TRAIL

SEPULCHER MTN. TRAIL

CLAGETT BUTTE TRAIL

BEAVER PONDS LOOP TRAIL

SNOW PASS

HOWARD EATON TRAIL

LAVA CREEK TRAIL

BUNSEN PEAK TRAIL

OSPREY FALLS TRAIL

1   0   1

*Electric Peak
and the Gardner River.*

ELECTRIC PEAK SPUR TRAIL
(3 miles, 5 km)

This is not a maintained trail and is only a marked route to assist hikers in navigation. The route is very steep and some scrambling must be done near the summit. The trail climbs 3,000 vertical feet and the summit of Electric Peak is 9 miles from the Glen Creek Trailhead. The view from the summit is superb and on a clear day you can see everything from the town of Gardiner, Montana to the Grand Tetons.

The spur trail up Electric Peak leaves the Sportsman Lake Trail-East about 6 miles from the Glen Creek Trailhead on the ridge above and north of the Gardner River crossing. The route follows the top of this ridge through open meadows until it reaches the Southeast Ridge of Electric Peak. Follow the Southeast Ridge on scree slopes until you are stopped by a band of rock about 150 vertical feet below the summit. Traverse down to the left (south) about 50 feet until you come to a break in the wall. Veer right (northwest) through this break and up a gully to regain the Southeast Ridge. Scramble along the ridge top to the summit. Careful hand and foot placements are important here as the rock is loose. To descend you will use the same route. *Map 2*

BUNSEN PEAK TRAIL
(2 miles 3 kilometers)

The hike up Bunsen Peak is an especially good short, steep trip. The view from the top is awesome at sunrise. The early sun turns the eastern slopes of nearby Electric Peak a glowing gold. Although it's only about a 1300 foot climb to Bunsen's summit, the view will make it seem much higher as you stare down the peak's north face and look out to the Yellowstone River Valley 3,000 feet below you.

Bunsen Peak is actually the eroded remains of an ancient volcano's cone. Don't let that keep you from taking the hike, it hasn't erupted in 50 million years. The peak is named for Robert Bunsen, who did early research on geysers. Bunsen Peak has been burned over by forest fires many times in the past, and it happened again in 1988. In its wake, we are left with a classic burn mosaic.

The trail starts at the entrance to the Bunsen Peak Road, 5 miles south of Mammoth. Walk up the Bunsen Road a short distance and watch for the trail markers leading up the slope on your left. The trail climbs through sagebrush and burned pine and fir. There is National Park Service radio relaying equipment near the top. *Map 3*

OSPREY FALLS TRAIL
(2 miles, 3 kilometers)

The Osprey Falls Trail starts on the Bunsen Peak Road about 3 miles from the road's one-way entrance. The Bunsen Road is dirt and gravel, steep and winding, and closed after wet weather. When it is open, it's navigable by passenger cars. The trail starts right at the rim of Sheepeater Canyon and drops 800 vertical feet down a series of switchbacks to the canyon bottom. Sheepeater Canyon was named for the Sheepeater Indians, a band of the Shoshone tribe that frequented this region of the park. Once at the bottom of this narrow, deep canyon, the trail follows the Gardner River up to the base of Osprey Falls. Don't approach too closely to the cliffs at the base of the falls, as the rock is wet and loose. The Osprey Falls is a memorable sight; the Gardner River plunges over a 150 foot drop directly in front of you while the vertical cliffs of the canyon tower above your head. *Map 3*

LAVA CREEK TRAIL

Lava Creek Trailhead to:

Mouth of Lava Creek	1 miles	1.5 km
Undine Falls	3	5
Lava Creek picnic area	3.5	6
Jct. with Blacktail Creek Trail	6	9.5

The Lava Creek Trailhead is at the end of a service road behind the Mammoth school and softball diamond. The entrance to the service road is across from the Mammoth Campground. The trail starts at a footbridge that crosses the Gardner River. The trail then follows the Gardner River upstream to the mouth of Lava Creek. Look for signs of beaver working in this area. The trail now follows Lava Creek upstream at the bottom of the rock walls of Mount Everts on your left. As you approach Undine Falls, you enter a forest and the trail begins to climb steeply.

Undine is a beautiful double falls, picturesque enough to have once graced the cover of National Geographic Magazine. Once above the falls, you'll have several choices: 1) You can cross Lava Creek and walk to the Undine Falls parking area. 2) You can continue to follow the trail another ½ mile to a short cutoff to the Lava Creek picnic area,where you can cross Lava Creek on the highway bridge. 3) Past this point, the Lava Creek Trail turns into the Howard Eaton Trail. You can continue on this through meadows and past Blacktail Ponds to the Blacktail Creek Trail Junction. *Maps 3, 4*

BEAVER PONDS LOOP TRAIL
(5 miles, 8 kilometers)

The Beaver Ponds Trail travels through stands of Douglas fir and aspen and through meadows of grass, sage and other flowering plants to a series of ponds dammed by (you guessed it) beavers. Unfortunately for us, the beavers go about most of their above surface activity in the early morning and late evening. consequently, most people miss seeing nature's answer to the Army corps of Engineers as the beaver repair and improve their log dams and lodges. Due to the lower elevation here, the scenery along the trail is often most interesting in late spring or during the fall. Because the snow leaves earlier and comes later, the larger animals migrate here and stay from October to June. Chances of seeing them at this time are excellent. The flowers (such as bitterroot and primrose) are already blooming in May and June, and in the fall the aspen leaves turn a golden yellow. Another good reason for hiking this trail in spring or fall is because it can be a hot, dry hike during the summer. Black bears are occasionally spotted in this locale, so make noise while hiking. Pronghorn also frequent the lower portions of this trail during the summer; but the same noise that scares bears usually scares pronghorn too.

One of the park's few short loop trails, the Beaver Ponds Trail, starts in Mammoth in the gulch between Liberty Cap and a grey stone residence building. This gulch is the drainage for Clematis Creek. The trail travels up the gulch, gaining about 400 feet in ½ mile, until it hits the junction with the Sepulcher Mountain Trail. Here the Beaver Ponds Trail turns right (north) and continues climbing to a good vantage point. The ponds are about 1.5 miles further, for a total of 2.5 miles from the trailhead. From the ponds, the trail travels through sagebrush for 2 miles to the old Gardiner Road. Along this section there are good views of the steep bare slopes of Mt. Everts to the east and prominent Sheep Mtn. to the north. The trail continues to follow the old road until it ends behind the Mammoth Motor Inn. *Map 3*

FAN CREEK TRAIL

From Fawn Pass Trailhead (milepost 22, Highway 191) to:

Jct. with Fan Creek Trail	1.5 miles	2.5 km
Jct. with Sportsman Lake Trail	8.5	13.5

The Fan Creek Trail is a relatively new fishing access trail and won't be shown on topographic maps put out before 1980. The Fan Creek Trail starts at the Fawn pass Trailhead and follows the Fawn pass Trail for 1.5 miles. At the junction, the Fan Creek Trail turns northeast and heads up through the meadows of Fan Creek.

Moose are often seen in the willows along the creek. At mile 4.5 Fan Creek must be waded. This crossing can be thigh to waist deep until early July. At about the 6 mile mark the North and East Fork of Fan Creek converge. The trail follows the North Fork until it reaches the junction with the Sportsman Lake Trail. From this junction it is about 2.5 miles to Sportsman Lake.

The Fan Creek Trail can be combined with other trails to make a long loop hike over the Gallatin Range. By using the Sportsman Lake Trail, Fawn Pass Trail, and the Fan Creek Trail the distance will be: 43 miles if you start at Glen Creek Trailhead on the Mammoth-Norris Road, or 42 miles if you start at Fawn Pass Trailhead on Highway 191.

The upper portion of the Fan Creek Trail may require hiking parties of 4 or more and off trail hiking may be prohibited. Check at a N.P.S. ranger station or visitor center for details. *Map 2*

SEPULCHER MOUNTAIN TRAIL

From Glen Creek Trailhead (5 miles south of Mammoth) to:

Sepulcher Mtn. Trail Jct.	3 miles	5 km
Summit of Sepulcher Mtn.	5	8
Jct. with Claggett Butte Trail	8	13
Jct. with Beaver Ponds Trail	8.7	14
Clematis Creek/Liberty Cap Trailhead	9.2	15
Glen Creek Trailhead	12	19

The Sepulcher Mountain Trail can be turned into one of the best loop hikes in the park, providing a little bit of every kind of scenery Yellowstone has to offer. This 9,652 ft peak is named for the strangely shaped formations of volcanic rock near its summit. To some morbid soul these looked like grave markers or sepulchers. There are a number of route combinations that will take you to the mountain's summit. The easiest of these starts at the Glen Creek Trailhead and follows the Sportsman Lake Trail to its junction with the Sepulcher Mtn. Trail. From the junction, the Sepulcher Mtn. Trail climbs 2,300 feet through open meadows that are filled with flowers during June and July. Another route starts at Mammoth Hot Springs at the Clematis Creek Trailhead, near Liberty Cap, and climbs 3,400 feet up the forested slopes of Sepulcher's north face. Either way you choose to ascend, you can make a loop hike out of the trail by hiking down the other way and going through Snow Pass to reach your respective trailhead. (See Map no. 2 for a clearer picture of this). *Maps 2, 3*

LOWER YELLOWSTONE RIVER AREA

The area around the lower Yellowstone River (between Tower Falls and Gardiner, Montana) is one of relatively low elevation. While most of Yellowstone Park is about 7,000 - 8,000 feet above sea level, most of the lower Yellowstone is between 5,000 - 6,000 feet. The difference in temperature, plant life, animal distribution, and rock formation is very noticeable.

Because this area is lower, summer comes earlier and winter later. Stands of aspen, cottonwood, Douglas fir, limber pine and Rocky Mountain juniper grow here instead of the vast and dense lodgepole pine forests of the higher elevations. You'll even see cactus along the lower portions of the Yellowstone River and Rescue Creek Trails. When winter comes and the rest of the park is buried in deep snow, the lower Yellowstone River area has relatively little snow. That makes it an attractive wintering spot for Yellowstone's transient mammals. Bison, elk, pronghorn, mule deer, bighorn sheep and coyotes are densely congregated in this area from November to May. But even though the snow and cold aren't as severe here as the rest of the park, it's by no means a tropical paradise for those wintering animals. Temperatures are constantly below freezing; the snow crusts and hardens making grazing an energy sapping, inefficient chore. With all these hungry animals, there is a lot of competition for the available food. The trees are browsed as far up as the animals can reach and this obvious "browse line" is evident all year. Despite the cold and crowding most animals make it; but some don't. They die due to old age or complications caused by lack of food and the cold, just as animals have been doing for thousands and thousands of years. Those that die are food for insects, coyotes, bears, ravens, magpies and others. Parts of the animals that aren't immediately consumed will eventually decompose, and their bodies' elements will be recycled back into the soil, providing nutrients for plants and, thus eventually, other animals. Come spring, the bones and antlers will be all that remain, but these too will disappear as they also decompose or are nibbled away by calcium-seeking rodents (or are stolen by illegal antler hunters).

The rock formations in this area also differ from the predominantly volcanic material that covers most of the rest of Yellowstone. The gneiss and schist exposed here is some of the oldest rock in the park. Formed during Precambrian times over 2.5 billion years ago, these rocks were originally granite, slate and sandstone until they were changed and crumpled by heat and pressure. The north face of Hellroaring Mtn. exposes a 2,000 foot block of this metamorphic rock which can be viewed from the Hellroaring Creek Trail.

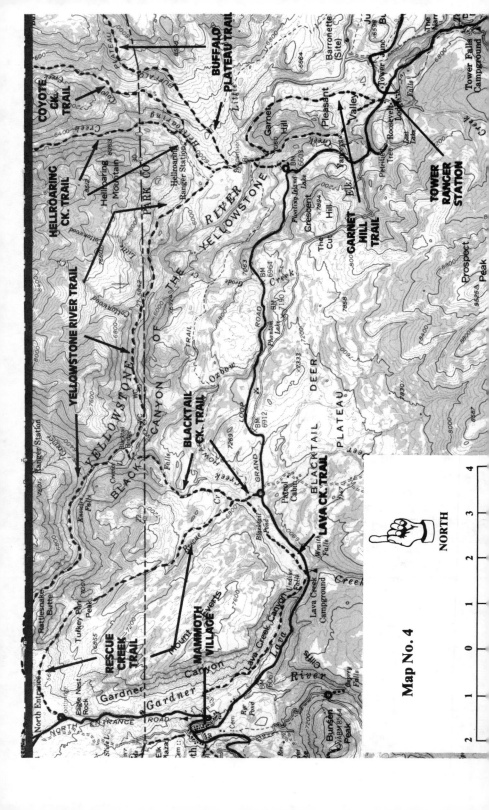

Map No. 4

YELLOWSTONE RIVER TRAIL

The Yellowstone River Trail travels from Hellroaring Trailhead to Gardiner, Montana. The trail follows the Yellowstone River, passing a variety of interesting features along its 18 mile length. For most of the way the river flows through the Black Canyon of the Yellowstone. This canyon is over 1,000 feet deep, and in many places the dark canyon walls rise vertically from the water's edge. The western end of the canyon contains Knowles Falls, a 15 foot drop of the Yellowstone River. You'll find that when a river this size drops even a mere fifteen feet, the result is still impressive.

Wildlife is abundant here from late fall through early spring. Bison, elk, bighorn sheep, pronghorn, mule deer and coyotes all congregate in this area during the cold months. By mid June these animals will have moved to higher elevations. and until November they will be scarce along the lower Yellowstone.

Because this trail goes through some of the lowest elevations in the park, it's a good place to hike when other spots are too cold, wet or mosquito infested. This can be a hot hike during the summer (especially Knowles Falls to Gardiner) and even during early fall, so plan to do the majority of your hiking early and late in the day. *Map 4*

From Hellroaring Trailhead to:

Yellowstone River Suspension Bridge	1 miles	1.5 km
Hellroaring Ck. Trail Jct.	1.5	2.5
Hellroaring Ck. footbridge	2	3
Hellroaring Ck. stockbridge	3	5
Cottonwood Creek	6	9.5
Blacktail Ck. Trail Jct.	10	16
Crevice Creek	11	17.5
Knowles Falls	11.5	18.5
Gardiner, Montana	18.5	29.5

Starting at Hellroaring Trailhead, 3.5 miles from Tower on the Tower-Mammoth Road, the trail descends a series of switchbacks to the Yellowstone River. The descent is about 600 vertical feet in a mile, which won't seem too important for those going down, but you'll remember each of those 600 feet if you have to trudge up them after a long day of hiking with a full pack. After crossing the suspension bridge, the trail leads into open sageland and continues to the junction with the Hellroaring Creek Trail. (If you follow the Hellroaring Creek Trail north, you'll come to a stockbridge across Hellroaring Creek. You'll also meet the Coyote Creek Trail). Continuing on the Yellowstone River Trail, you'll proceed to the Hellroaring Creek footbridge, about ½ mile further. This will be the last water available until Little Cottonwood Creek.

From Hellroaring Creek the trail climbs open slopes to a ridge above the walls of the Black Canyon. Here, from about 400 feet above, the view of the Yellowstone River and its canyon is simply inspiring. Gazing out over such a large river so unchanged and unspoiled by man is a marvelous feeling. The trail gradually descends to Little Cottonwood Creek and then on to Cottonwood Creek. From the creek, the trail follows the river closely, while directly across the water the immense black walls of the canyon rise prominently.

Knowles Falls

Four miles from Cottonwood Creek the Yellowstone River Trail meets the Blacktail Creek Trail. (From this point the Blacktail Creek Trail heads south, crosses the suspension bridge and climbs 1,100 feet out to the Mammoth-Tower Road). The Yellowstone River Trail heads west from the junction, past Crevice Lake and on to Crevice Creek. A bridge takes you over this delightful, tumbling stream to the junction with the Crevice Creek Trail. (The Crevice Creek Trail climbs 2,000 feet in 2 miles through open sage and grassland to the park's north boundary. During the summer this is a hot, strenuous hike).

After the Crevice Creek junction, the Yellowstone River Trail climbs steeply up, over and down a ridge to a point downstream from Knowles Falls, where a good view of the falls is available. From the falls, the trail again follows the Yellowstone River until the river enters another narrow stretch of the canyon. The trail climbs up and over this section. Once back by the river, there is a good view upstream of the canyon and of a large cave carved out of the canyon wall across the river from you.

From this point to Gardiner (6 miles away), the trail travels above and away from the river; so make certain to fill your water bottles before starting on this section. Along this final section of trail the Yellowstone River has shaped some intriguing rock formations, and you'll be treated to a type of scenery most people don't associate with Yellowstone. The trail exits just north of the Yellowstone River Bridge in Gardiner. Check with the Mammoth Visitor Center for information on where to park your car at this end of the trail.

RESCUE CREEK TRAIL

From Blacktail Trailhead (7 miles east of Mammoth) to:

Jct. with Rescue Creek Trail	0.7 miles	1 km
Turkey Pen Peak	5	8
North Entrance Road	8	13

The Rescue Creek Trail travels from the Blacktail Trailhead on the Mammoth-Tower Road to the trailhead located about 1 mile south of the North Entrance Station. From the Blacktail Trailhead, the route follows the Blacktail Creek Trail for the first ¾ of a mile. The Rescue Creek Trail veers off to the left at this point and starts to climb gradually. It follows Rescue Creek upstream for a little over a mile then climbs moderately up a low grassy hill. From this point, it's all downhill as the trail descends 1,400 feet in the remaining 6 miles. The trail passes by Turkey Pen Peak and Rattlesnake Butte on its way to the Gardner River Footbridge. The vegetation along this pleasant downhill ramble includes sagebrush, aspen, Douglas fir and a variety of early blooming flowers. Use discretion in choosing a spot to sit down for a rest, or you may inadvertently encounter the prickly pear cactus. From November through May wildlife viewing is very good with elk, mule deer, coyote, bighorn sheep, pronghorn and an occasional grizzly bear spotted along this section. During the summer this is a hot dry hike with Rescue Creek as the only source of water until you reach the Gardner River. Large animals are scarce along this trail during the summer, as are mosquitoes. *Map 4*

BLACKTAIL CREEK TRAIL

Blacktail Trailhead (7 miles east of Mammoth) to:

Jct. with Rescue Creek Trail	.7 miles	1.0 km
Blacktail Suspension Bridge	3.7	6.0
Yellowstone River Trail	4.0	6.5
Knowles Falls	5.5	9.0

The Blacktail Creek Trail travels from the Mammoth-Tower Road to the Yellowstone River and the Yellowstone River Trail. The trail follows Blacktail Creek as it descends 1,100 feet in 4 miles with about 900 of those feet dropping away in the last mile and a half. The trail passes down among rolling, grassy hills that bloom with wildflowers such as bitterroot and wild orchids during June and early July. If you hike this trail before they hibernate in August, you'll probably also encounter a colony of Uinta ground squirrels. As the trail nears the river it enters a Douglas fir forest and continues down to the Blacktail Bridge. After crossing this large sturdy suspension bridge, the Blacktail Creek Trail continues a few hundred yards to the junction with the Yellowstone River Trail. From this junction it's about ¼ mile further to Crevice Lake and about 1.5 miles to Knowles Falls via the Yellowstone River Trail. *Map 4*

BUFFALO PLATEAU TRAIL

The Buffalo Plateau Trail offers a wide variety of scenery to go along with a lengthy strenuous hike. The Trail travels from the Hellroaring Creek Trail up to the Buffalo Plateau and Buffalo Fork Creek, north of the park boundary. It descends back into the park and joins the Slough Creek Trail. The upper portions of this trail were burned in the fires of **1988**, but shouldn't detract from your hiking experience if you don't mind black trees, better views, and more undergrowth. From the Hellroaring Creek Trail you'll climb about 3,000 feet in 7 miles through open sage slopes, stands of Douglas, and sub-alpine meadows. *Map 4*

Hellroaring Trailhead (3.5 miles west of Tower Jct.) to:

Jct. with Buffalo Plateau Trail	1.4 miles	2.2 km
Buffalo Plateau Patrol Cabin	9	14.5
Poacher Trail	11.5	18.5
Buffalo Fork	13	21
Slough Creek Trail	20	32
Slough Creek Trailhead	22	35

The Buffalo Plateau Trail is easy to follow from the Hellroaring Trail junction to the Buffalo Plateau Patrol Cabin near the north boundary; after that it's not so easily followed as it receives little use. From the cabin, the trail travels about 1.5 miles north to an old east-west running poacher's trail which is now maintained and well marked by the U.S. Forest Service. This area does receive more precipitation and stock use than the lower portions of the trail. This can make for some muddy hiking conditions. Once on the poachers' trail, you follow it east as it descends 1900 feet to the scenic meadow along Buffalo Fork Creek. To loop back into Yellowstone, follow the trail that leads south from the meadows on the east side of the creek. This trail will climb above and away from Buffalo Fork Creek and onto the lower slopes of Anderson Mountain. From mid September through mid October this area is an excellent spot for watching elk and listening to them bugle. The trail descends from Anderson Mountain down to the Slough Creek Valley. To reach the Slough Creek Trail you must cross Slough Creek, which is slow and calf deep most of the summer but can be swift and waist deep before mid July. The Slough Creek Trail continues 2 miles to the Slough Creek Trailhead.

COYOTE CREEK TRAIL

From Hellroaring Trailhead to:

Hellroaring Trail/Coyote Ck. Trail Jct.	3 miles	5 km
North boundary of Yellowstone	6.5	10.5
Jct. with U.S.F.S. Hellroaring Trail	11	17.5

Start at the Hellroaring Trailhead (3.5 miles from Tower Junction on the Mammoth-Tower Road) and follow the Hellroaring Creek Trail to the vicinity of the Hellroaring Patrol Cabin, approximately 3 miles from the trailhead. The Coyote Creek Trail leaves the Hellroaring Trail and veers to the northeast. The trail travels through sage meadows and open stands of Douglas Fir. The views of the Washburn Range and the Yellowstone River Valley to the south are very nice as you climb up the open hillsides that lead into the spruce-fir-pine forest of the plateau. By the time you reach the north boundary you will have climbed approximately 1500 vertical feet from Hellroaring Creek. It is possible to continue north from the boundary, gradually descending through the forest, to the Gallatin National Forest section of the Hellroaring Creek Trail. This can be followed south back to Yellowstone Park and Hellroaring Trailhead, making for a loop hike. The section of trail in the National Forest receives a great deal of stock use, and more precipitation than the lower sections of trail, an can be quite mucky for hiking. *Map 4*

HELLROARING CREEK TRAIL

The Hellroaring Creek Trail travels from the Mammoth-Tower Road to the park's north boundary, and continues into the Gallatin National Forest. The trail follows Hellroaring Creek through sageland and stands of Douglas fir and past rock outcrops over 2 billion years old. Pronghorn, elk, mule deer, moose and bison may all be seen along the Hellroaring Creek Trail from November to June. During the summer chances aren't very good for seeing large animals, although moose and mule deer are sometimes spotted early in the morning.

The confluence of Hellroaring Creek and the Yellowstone River is a delightful spot. There is the cold clear rushing water of the creek, the deep surging river, a sandy beach and the sheer walls of the Black Canyon of the Yellowstone. Osprey nest in these cliffs and are frequently seen flying over the river looking for trout. Although there is no marked trail to this spot, it can be easily reached by walking downstream through the sagebrush along Hellroaring Creek from the junction with the Yellowstone River Trail. *Map 4*

Hellroaring Trailhead to:

	miles	km
Yellowstone River Suspension Bridge	1	1.5
Jct. with Buffalo Plateau Trail	1.5	2.5
Jct. with Yellowstone River Trail	2	3.2
Hellroaring Creek Stockbridge	3.5	.5
North boundary	7	11.2

The Hellroaring Trailhead is 3.5 miles from Tower Junction on the Mammoth-Tower Road and is just north of Floating Island Lake. The trail descends a series of switchbacks, dropping about 600 feet in a mile to the suspension bridge over the Yellowstone River. The trail then travels through sagebrush, past the Buffalo Plateau Trail junction, to the junction with the Yellowstone River Trail.

From the junction, the Hellroaring Creek Trail heads north up the forested valley of Hellroaring Creek. Hellroaring Mountain looms high above on your left and Buffalo Plateau rises to your right. About a mile past the junction a patrol cabin will come into view across the creek. From here it is ½ mile further to the stockbridge over Hellroaring Creek. The bridge crosses over a calm, deep pool of the creek. Look down while crossing and you may be able to see cutthroat trout swimming in the clear water below you. (Once across the bridge, there is a trail leading south along the west side of the creek back to the Yellowstone River Trail). From the bridge, the Hellroaring Creek Trail continues north through the rocky forested valley to the park's north boundary. The trail continues into the Gallatin National Forest where several long loop hikes are possible. Consult a U.S.G.S. 15 minute map of the Mt. Wallace, Montana Quadrangle for the location of these trails.

TOWER AREA

This section is devoted to those trails starting in the vicinity of Tower Junction and Tower Fall. The area offers a number of interesting short hikes, most of which are conveniently located for people staying at the Roosevelt Lodge or the Tower Campground. The main points of interest in the area are Tower Fall, the Grand Canyon of the Yellowstone and the petrified trees. Good views of the Grand Canyon are available from the Specimen Ridge Trail, the Yellowstone River Picnic Area Trail and the Agate Creek Trail. The petrified trees are located mainly on Specimen Ridge, away from any maintained trails; although you can see a petrified tree from your car at the Petrified Tree Road.

The elevation and climate of the Tower Area is similar to that of the Lower Yellowstone Area: lower, warmer, and drier than most of the park. Thus, the larger mammals such as bison, elk, pronghorn, mule deer and bighorn sheep are more abundant here from the fall through the spring than they are during the summer. Moose may be seen at anytime throughout the summer as may an occasional black bear. Because this area is drier, mosquitoes usually aren't as bad, and they thin out sooner than in other places in the park.

TOWER CREEK TRAIL
(2.8 miles, 4.5 kilometers)

The Tower Creek Trail travels from the entrance of Tower Campground up through the forested canyon of Tower Creek. This area was burned by the fires in 1988 and offers a good look at the relationship between a burned area and a stream. Notice how burned trees that have fallen in the stream change the course of a stream and add new eddies and pools. This trail is used mainly by people interested in fishing, but it also offers a pleasant hike along a rushing mountain stream and the chance to spot kingfishers, water ouzels and an occasional moose. *Map 5*

TOWER FALLS TRAIL
(0.5 miles, 0.8 km)

This trail starts at the parking area adjacent to the Tower Falls General Store. After a hundred yards there is an overlook of the falls which is as far as most people go. For those that continue down to the base of this 132 foot falls, the view is much more impressive. The trail descends a total of about 200 feet on a series of switchbacks. *Map 5*

YELLOWSTONE RIVER PICNIC AREA TRAIL
(2 miles, 3 km)

This short easy trail travels from the Yellowstone River Picnic Area (1.5 miles east of Tower Junction on the Northeast Entrance Road) to the Specimen Ridge Trail. A spectacular view of the Grand Canyon and the Yellowstone River awaits those who take this often overlooked hike. The trail parallels the canyon for most of its 2 miles and bighorn sheep can occasionally be seen during fall and early summer. *Map 5*

AGATE CREEK TRAIL
(7.5 miles, 12 km)

The Agate Creek Trail provides panoramic views of the Washburn Range and access to a remote section of the Grand Canyon of the Yellowstone. The trail starts at the Specimen Ridge Trailhead (2.5 miles east of Tower Jct.) and follows the Specimen Ridge Trail for the first 3 miles. After veering south off the Specimen Ridge Trail the Agate Creek Trail contours around the Quartz Creek drainage through open terrain, then drops steeply down about 1,100 feet to the confluence of Agate Creek and the Yellowstone River. The confluence is a beautiful spot and worth the long hike. *Map 5*

LOST LAKE TRAIL

From Roosevelt Lodge to:

Jct. with Trail to Tower Falls	0.6 miles	1 km
Lost Lake	0.8	1.3
Petrified Tree	2	3
Tower Ranger Station	4	6.5

The Lost Lake Trail starts behind the Roosevelt Lodge at Tower Junction and leads up through the forested hillside until it comes to a trail junction. The trail to the left (east) leads eventually to Tower Fall. The Lost Lake trail continues to the right (west) and reaches Lost Lake in .2 mile. Waterfowl are frequently seen in the lake, beaver occasionally. From the lake the trail contours around the hillside down to the Petrified Tree Parking Area where you may view petrified trees behind iron fences. Without the fences these would probably be no more than Petrified Stumps, due to years of plundering by thoughtless specimen gatherers. To loop back to Tower Ranger Station, follow the trail at the northeast end of the parking lot. This trail climbs up to open sage hill tops with good views of the Buffalo Plateau. This is also a good area to look for hawks during spring and fall migrations. The trail descends to Tower Ranger Station. From here it is about ¼ mile back to Roosevelt Lodge. *Map 5*

ROOSEVELT LODGE TO TOWER FALL
(3.6 miles 5.8 kilometers)

This is a good trail for people staying at Roosevelt Lodge or Tower Campground who wish to walk between the two locations instead of drive. This trail, which climbs about 400 vertical feet, offers a good blend of views and a variety of terrain. Starting behind Roosevelt Lodge, on the trail to Lost Lake, you follow the Lost Lake Trail up the hill for approximately .6 mile to a trail junction. Lost Lake is to the right (west) and Tower Fall is to the left (south east). Turning left, you will reach an overlook of Lost Creek Falls after another .6 mile. The trail continues east through forest another .4 mile where a heavily used horse trail will veer off to the north, down to the Roosevelt corral. You'll want to continue heading east on the trail to Tower Fall. The next stretch of trail travels along the side of a ridge through meadows and aspen groves with tremendous views of the surrounding area. As the trail nears Tower Creek it descends abruptly 200 vertical feet to a footbridge over the creek. This will put you on the entrance road to Tower Campground; the campground is up the road to the right and Tower Fall and general store are down the road to the left. *Map 5*

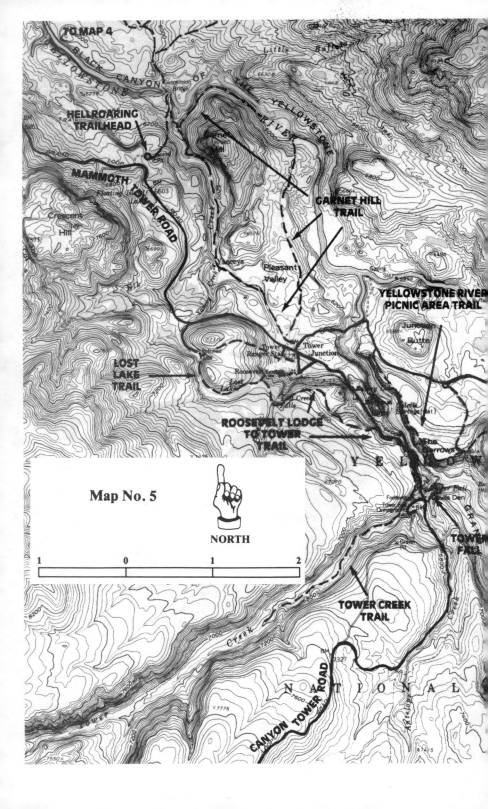

PETRIFIED
TREES

SPECIMEN
RIDGE
TRAIL

AGATE
CREEK TRAIL

TO MAP 7

GARNET HILL LOOP TRAIL

From Tower Ranger Station to:

Yancey's Creek	1.5 miles	2.5 km
Junction with spur trail to		
Hellroaring Creek Trail	3.5	5.5
Tower Ranger Station	7.5	12

The Garnet Hill Trail is a good loop hike travelling through a variety of terrain without a great deal of elevation loss and gain. The trail also provides access to the Hellroaring Creek and Yellowstone River Trails. On sunny summer days the last stretch of this trail can be pretty hot and dry. Start near Tower Junction and follow the stagecoach road west to Yancey's Creek and the stagecoach cookout area. The Garnet Hill trail goes to the right just before you reach the cookout area. For the next 2 miles the trail follows Elk Creek through meadows where mule deer are often spotted during spring and fall. (At the junction to the Hellroaring Trail, you may want to take a ½ mile side trip to the suspension bridge over the Yellowstone River, or you may want to reach the Hellroaring Creek area or the Yellowstone River Trail; if so, turn to the left and follow the trail across Elk Creek and down to the suspension bridge). The Garnet Hill Trail contours around Garnet Hill, through forest, until it breaks out into the open sage hills of Pleasant Valley.

After about 1.5 miles of hiking through Pleasant Valley (a very nice walk late in the evening) you will hit the junction with the stage road that you started on. It is now about ¾ of a mile back to Tower Ranger Station. *Map 5*

Petrified Trees

Probably the easiest access to the petrified trees of Specimen Ridge is from a service road that leaves the Northeast Entrance Road a few hundred yards west of the Lamar River Bridge and about 5 miles from Tower Junction. Park on this service road and walk south, following the ridge that is just west of the west fork of Crystal Creek. The right (west) side of this ridge is forested and the left (east) side is open meadows. Near the top of this ridge, just inside the forest on the right side, you will find some standing petrified trees. This is a very steep hike and there is no maintained trail. You must climbs about 800 vertical feet in 1.5 miles. The best way to do this trip is by joining the ranger-naturalist led hike to the petrified trees. This meets at Tower Ranger Station. Check there for details on the hike and for a detailed map showing the locations of the petrified trees. Remember: it is unlawful, and bad etiquette, to remove anything from the petrified trees. Map 5

SPECIMEN RIDGE TRAIL

The Specimen Ridge Trail travels from the trailhead (2.5 miles east of Tower Junction on the Northeast Entrance Road) to the Lamar River trailhead. This trail offers sub alpine meadows filled with wildflowers and sweeping vistas of the park. Although the trail runs near petrified trees, you can't actually see them from the Specimen Ridge Trail. To reach the fabled 27 layers of exposed petrified trees requires steep off-trail travel either up from the Lamar Valley, or down from the summit of Amethyst Mountain. *Maps 5, 7*

From Trailhead (2.5 miles east of Tower Jct.) to:

Grand Canyon of the Yellowstone	1 miles	1.5 km
Jct. with Agate Creek Trail	3	5
Summit of Amethyst Mountain (9,614')	11.5	18
Lamar River ford	16	26
Lamar Trailhead	17.5	28

Starting from the east, the Specimen Ridge Trail climbs moderately through sagebrush to the edge of the Grand Canyon of the Yellowstone. This spot provides a fine view upstream of the Yellowstone River and the magnificent canyon it has carved for itself. From the edge of the canyon the trail climbs more steeply, about 600 feet in the next 2 miles to the junction with the Agate Creek Trail. The Specimen Ridge Trail continues to climb through sage and grass meadows where elk are often spotted feeding during early morning. As the trail ascends, you'll notice the difference in vegetation, not only in the trees, but the flowering plants as well. When the summit of Amethyst Mountain is reached you will be at the trail's highest point and will have gained about 3,400 feet in elevation from the trailhead.

From the summit of Amethyst Mountain, the Specimen Ridge Trail descends steeply about 2,800 feet through forest and meadows (where grouse are often encountered) to the Lamar River. Here a knee deep ford is required (can be over waist deep and not passable before mid July). Once across the river, the trail travels through sagebrush to the Lamar River Trail which you'll follow to the Lamar Trailhead on the Northeast Entrance Road.

NORTHEAST CORNER

The Northeast Corner of Yellowstone National Park contains wide open Slough Creek Valley, the forested valley of Pebble Creek and the rugged mountains that surround the two. Trails follow both of these valleys and the Bliss Pass Trail makes a strenuous, but scenic, connecting route between them. This area is best enjoyed after late July, when the snow has left the passes, the mosquitoes have thinned out in the forest, and the streams have subsided and become easier to cross.

SLOUGH CREEK TRAIL

The Slough (pronounced "slew") Creek Trail travels from Slough Creek Campground to the park's north boundary, following Slough Creek through a broad, grassy valley most of the way. The best time to see wildlife along this trail is during the fall (late September and October) when the elk gather in the valley and the surrounding low ridges for the mating season and the coming winter. On fall mornings and evenings the bugling of bull elk can be heard as they challenge a far off rival. During the summer, moose are occasionally seen in the valley, as are trumpeter swans. *Map 6*

From Slough Creek Trailhead to:

Buffalo Plateau Trail Junction	2 miles	3 km
McBride Lake	3	5
Bliss Pass Trail Junction	8	13
North Boundary	11	17.5

The Slough Creek Trail starts from the gravel road leading to Slough Creek Campground, and is reached about ½ mile before the campground. From the trailhead, the Slough Creek Trail climbs gradually through stands of Douglas fir up to an open area where there is a good view of Cutoff Mountain to the northeast. The trail then descends to the broad open valley of Slough Creek. This area is known as the "First Meadow" and here the Buffalo Plateau Trail turns off to the north. From this junction, McBride Lake is located across the creek to the northeast in a rocky forested area.

From the junction the Slough Creek Trail continues up the valley, leaving the creek as it climbs a 200 foot ridge and then descends the other side to what is known as the "Second Meadows." The trail again nears the creek at the junction with the Bliss Pass Trail. The Slough Creek Trail continues north through grassy meadows and forest to the park's north boundary. The Silvertip Ranch (privately owned) is just north of the boundary in the Gallatin National Forest. You may see the horse drawn wagons of the ranch operating on the Slough Creek Trail. There are many trails branching off the Slough Creek Trail north of the park which provide opportunities for long loop hikes. For trails in this area consult the 15 minute topographic maps of Mt. Wallace and Cutoff Mountain or a U.S.F.S map.

70

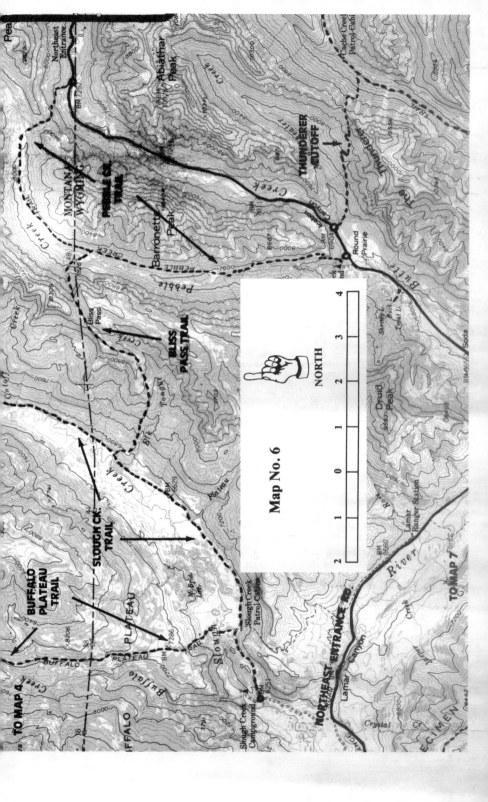

Map No. 6

NORTH

2   1   0   1   2   3   4

PEBBLE CREEK TRAIL

The Pebble Creek Trail travels through a glacial valley lined with rugged peaks rising to over 10,000 feet. The valley is mostly forest with lodgepole pine, Engleman spruce and subalpine fir. There are some extensive meadow areas in the upper Pebble Creek valley. These meadows contain blooming cinquefoil, geranium, lupine and other flowers during July and early August. Elk are frequently seen coming down into these meadows to feed during summer evenings and moose may occasionally be seen feeding on the willows along the banks of Pebble Creek. Mosquitoes may be quite numerous along Pebble Creek until early August, but shouldn't be bad enough to deter you from hiking through this scenic valley.

The trail travels from Pebble Creek Campground to the Warm Creek Picnic Area. Starting from the picnic area is the shortest way to get to the scenic upper valley of Pebble Creek; although this route does require a steep 1,100 foot climb.

Pebble Creek Trailhead (200 yards east of Pebble Creek Bridge on the Northeast Entrance Road) to:

Jct. with Bliss Pass Trail	6.6 miles	10.5 km
Upper Meadows	9.5	15.2
Warm Creek Picnic Area	12	19

On the west side, the trail starts at either Pebble Creek Campground or Pebble Creek Trailhead. The two trails join together after a short distance. The trail then climbs 500 feet on a series of switchbacks to a small meadow. Most normal people will rest here while taking in the spectacular view of the Thunderer to the southeast. The trail then parallels Pebble Creek through the forest above until about 3 miles from the trailhead where it makes two crossings of the creek in 200 yards. These crossings can be thigh deep and very swift before early July. Later in the summer Pebble Creek subsides to about calf deep.

From the crossings, the trail climbs up and away from the creek for another 3 miles until it meets the Bliss Pass Trail alongside a lovely little meadow. Further on, the Pebble Creek Trail makes another crossing and then enters the Upper Meadows. From the meadows there are good views of Cutoff Mountain (west), Wolverine Peak (north) and Sunset and Meridian Peaks (east). These peaks are summer range for bighorn sheep. The trail turns south and makes another crossing of Pebble Creek at the east end of the meadows. It then climbs about 200 feet to a ridge top where there is an excellent view of the sheer north face of Abiathar Peak. The trail now winds down through forest, dropping 1,100 feet in 1.5 miles to the Northeast Entrance Road. Along this last section of the trail there is a very nice view of the valley of Soda Butte Creek and Baronette Peak to the west. This impressive peak was named after "Yellowstone Jack" Baronette, a mountain man, guide, army scout, assistant superintendent of the park, and builder of the first bridge over the Yellowstone River. The trail meets the road at Warm Creek Picnic Area which is about 1.5 miles from the Northeast Entrance Station. *Map 6*

BLISS PASS TRAIL

This trail travels from the Slough Creek Trail, over 9,350 foot Bliss Pass, to the Pebble Creek Trail. From the Pebble Creek side, the Bliss Pass Trail gains 1,400 feet; while from the Slough Creek side it rises 2,700 feet. The scenery from either side is impressive. *Map 6*

From junction with Pebble Creek Trail (6.6 miles from Pebble Creek Trailhead and 5.5 miles from Warm Creek Picnic Area) to:

Bliss Pass	2 miles	3 km
Jct. with Slough Creek Trail	6	9.5
Slough Creek Trailhead	14	22.5

This trail may be started at either Pebble Creek Trailhead, Warm Creek Picnic Area or Slough Creek Trailhead. Starting from the junction with the Pebble Creek Trail, the Bliss Pass Trail immediately fords Pebble Creek. This ford is usually calf deep after mid summer, but may be knee to thigh deep and swift during June snow melt. From the crossing, the trail ascends through a meadow where the trail may be hard to follow. If so, look for the orange markers at the edge of the forest to the north. From the meadows the trail climbs steeply through timber to the pass.

From the pass, the trail descends, steeply in some spots, through forest and meadow to the Slough Creek Trail. From this point it's 8 miles of relatively level hiking to the Slough Creek Trailhead.

TROUT LAKE TRAIL
(0.5 miles, 0.8 km)

This trail is used mainly by anglers and only on a day use basis, as there are no backcountry campsites on Trout Lake. The trail starts from a small pullout about 1.5 miles south of Pebble Creek Campground on the Northeast Entrance Road. The trail climbs about 150 feet through stands of Douglas fir to the lake. Waterfowl may occasionally be spotted, as can the lake's large rainbow trout when they rise to feed on the surface. Back in the 1880's the fish in Trout Lake were an important food source for the people of nearby Cooke City, Montana. As you might suspect, the angling techniques were anything but sporting. Spears, nets and gunpowder were all employed to illegally harvest Trout Lake's trout. Unfortunately at that time there was no National Park Service, and the people administering Yellowstone National Park had neither the personnel or the power to prevent this poaching. Fortunately things today have changed. *Map 6*

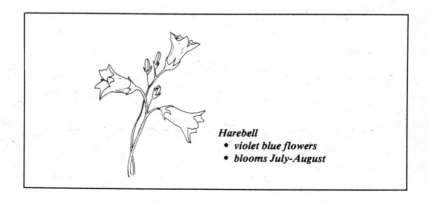

Harebell
- *violet blue flowers*
- *blooms July-August*

LAMAR RIVER AREA

As the title of the section suggests, the Lamar River is the central part of this huge wilderness area. The Lamar River carries away the water from the numerous valleys, mountains, and ridges; and consequently becomes quite deep and fast during early summer snow melt. The valley of the Lamar is also the area's main route of travel for both animals and people. In early summer bison and elk move up the valley from their wintering grounds to the high meadows, where they seek new plant growth and an escape from the hordes of biting insects. Most hikers traveling in this area will also follow the Lamar River for a portion of their hike as they too seek the high mountain meadows and the wildlife that live there.

Much of the Lamar Area was burned to varying degrees by the fires of 1988. As in other burned areas of the park, vegetation in the Lamar Area is growing back. Hiking through this area offers an excellent, though prolonged, opportunity to view the cycle of regrowth after a fire.

LAMAR RIVER TRAIL

The Lamar River Trail travels from the Lamar Trailhead to the Upper Lamar Patrol Station. The trail serves mainly as a connecting route for the numerous side trails heading to the high meadows, lakes and mountain passes of the park's east boundary. Much of this area was burned to varying degrees by the fires of 1988. The sections around Cache Creek and Miller Creek were intensely burned.

Upstream from Cache Creek to the end of the Lamar River Trail, the Lamar Valley is a narrow forested canyon; much different in appearance from the lower valley near the road which is open, wide and covered with sage and grass. Consequently, the majority of the Lamar River Trail is not a place to witness spectacular displays of wildlife, although occasional animals are still seen throughout the summer. Elk and bison winter in the valley downstream from Cache Creek and may be spotted there between October and early June. In summer they move up the valley to the higher elevations along open ridge tops above the valley floor, with only an occasional old bull bison lingering behind. *Map 7, 8*

From Lamar Trailhead (on Northeast Entrance Road about 4 miles west of Pebble Creek Campground) to:

Jct. with Cache Creek Trail	3.1 miles	5 km
Jct. with Miller Creek Trail	9.2	14.7
Cold Creek Junction	16	25.8
Upper Lamar Patrol Station	22	35

Hikers will start this trail at the Lamar Trailhead which is signed and provides a bridged crossing of Soda Butte Creek. Horse parties start at a parking area ¼ mile west of the Lamar Trailhead and must ford the creek. Leaving Lamar Trailhead and crossing the Soda Butte Creek Bridge, the Lamar Trail travels across flat meadows and soon passes the cutoff trail to the horse-use trailhead and the junction with the Specimen Ridge Trail. Further on, the trail passes the junction with the Cache Creek Trail, then descends about 200 feet to Cache Creek. Expect the crossing of Cache Creek to be anywhere from calf deep to knee deep after mid July. Before that time the crossing may be too deep and swift to cross safely.

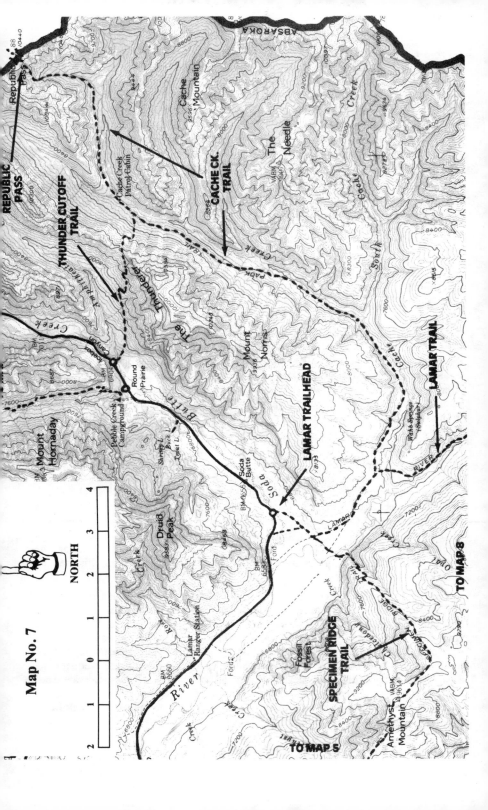

Map No. 7

NORTH

1 0 1 2 3 4

REPUBLIC PASS

THUNDER CUTOFF TRAIL

CACHE CK. TRAIL

LAMAR TRAILHEAD

LAMAR TRAIL

SPECIMEN RIDGE TRAIL

TO MAP 5

TO MAP 8

From Cache Creek, the Lamar River Trail parallels the Lamar River to Miller Creek and the junction with the Miller Creek Trail. After crossing Miller Creek (shallower than Cache Creek ford), the Lamar Trail travels alternately through forest and meadow and climbs up and over several side hills. Take time to sit and enjoy the refreshingly wild Lamar River as it rushes through one of these grassy meadows. Look for waterbirds and don't be surprised if you find a variety of wildflowers blooming in these spots during July and early August. At Cold Creek Junction, the Lamar River Trail connects with the Mist Creek Pass Trail and the Frost Lake Trail.

From Cold Creek Junction the Lamar River Trail continues to the Upper Lamar Patrol Station, following the Lamar River through a forested valley lined with mountain peaks.

CACHE CREEK TRAIL

From Junction with Lamar River Trail (3.1 miles from Lamar River Trailhead) to:

Jct. with Thunderer Cutoff Trail	11 miles	17.5 km
Republic Pass	16.5	26.5
Cooke City	21.5	34.5

From the junction with the Lamar River Trail, the Cache Creek Trail travels through sagebrush for the first mile then enters an area of intense burn from the fires of 1988. After about 2 miles, Death Gulch and Wahb Springs can be seen on the other side of Cache Creek. Death Gulch is accurately named. It contains a small thermal area that gives off a non-respirable gas that has killed everything from sparrows to bears. In fact, Wahb Springs is named after the bear in Ernest Thomphson Seton's story, "Biography of a Grizzly." In Seton's story, when Wahb knew his time was up, the huge old grizzly came to this deadly gulch to die.

The Cache Creek Trail continues to parallel the creek, crossing it twice, through forest and over numerous small side streams. The crossings of Cache Creek are calf deep and slippery after mid July. Near the confluence with South Cache Creek, the trail climbs up and away from Cache Creek and continues to the junction with the Thunderer Cutoff Trail. From this junction, the Cache Creek Trail continues about .3 miles to Cache Creek Patrol Cabin. Here the trail makes a shallow crossing of Cache Creek and then parallels an unnamed fork of the creek for about 3 miles. At this point the Cache Creek Trail turns north and follows a tributary of the unnamed fork. There is also a trail that continues along the unnamed fork which vanishes after about a mile, so don't get on this trail by mistake.

The Cache Creek Trail continues following the tributary, becoming steeper as it moves upstream. About 1 mile from Republic Pass the trail leaves the tributary and climbs directly to the pass. From Cache Creek Patrol Cabin the trail has climbed about 2,300 vertical feet to the 10,000 foot pass. The view from the pass is startling. Rugged snow streaked mountains appear on all sides, presenting a scene most people wouldn't think to associate with Yellowstone. Grizzlies frequent the area near Republic Pass; so be alert. From Republic Pass a Forest Service Trail continues about 5 miles down to the old Irma Mine road which comes out on Highway 212 at the east end of Cooke City. A topographic map will be helpful in negotiating this last section of trail. *Map 7*

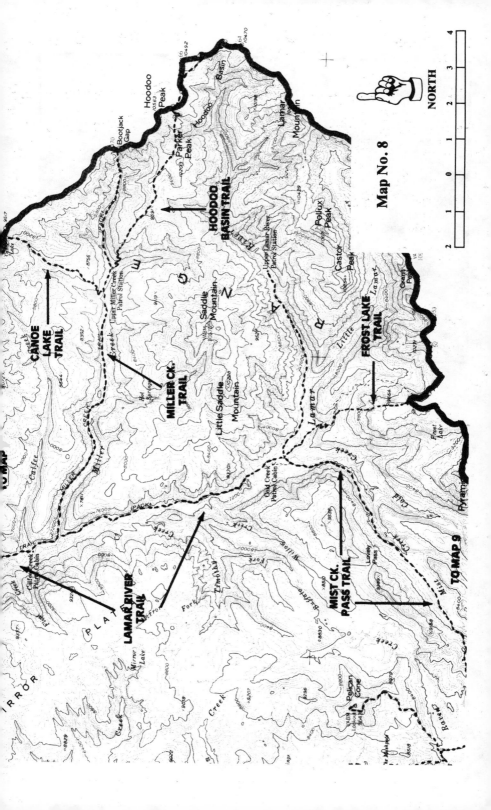

Map No. 8

NORTH

The Thunderer and Soda Butte Creek.

THUNDERER CUTOFF TRAIL

The Thunderer Cutoff Trail travels from the Northeast Entrance Road to upper Cache Creek by climbing 1,900 feet up and over the saddle between The Thunderer and Peak 10,300'. This trail is a good first leg of a semi-loop hike for either Republic Pass or the Cache Creek Trail. *Map 7*

From Trailhead (1 mile north of Pebble Creek Campground on the Northeast Entrance Road) to:

Pass (a.k.a. Chaw Pass)	4 miles	6.4 km
Cache Creek Trail	5.5	8.8
Republic Pass	11	17.6
Cooke City	17	27

From the trailhead you must immediately cross Soda Butte Creek which is only about calf deep after mid July. It may be possible to cross on a log jam about 75 yards upstream from the ford. Once across the creek, the trail winds through an open stand of lodgepole pine where there is an exceptional view of the sheer north face of The Thunderer. The trail soon begins to climb moderately, but steadily, to what is known locally as Chaw Pass. Unfortunately only occasional glimpses of spectacular Amphitheater Valley are available from the trail due to the trees; although there are good views, to the east, of the ridge tops above Cache Creek. From the pass, the trail descends about 1,000 feet in 1.5 miles to the junction with the Cache Creek Trail. From this junction it's 5.5 miles to Republic Pass or 14.5 miles down Cache Creek to the Lamar River Trailhead.

MILLER CREEK TRAIL

The Miller Creek Trail travels from the Lamar River Trail to the park's east boundary at Bootjack Gap. The trail follows Miller Creek through pine, spruce and fir forest, some of which was burned in the fires of 1988. The fire burned very intensely on the lower section of the trail, leaving almost a complete burn. The upper reaches of the trail burned less intensely, which resulted in more of a mosaic burn pattern. The Miller Creek Trail provides access to two very scenic spur trails: the Canoe Lake Trail and the Hoodoo Basin Trail. *Map 8*

From the junction with the Lamar River Trail (8.5 miles from Lamar Trailhead) to:

Jct. with Canoe Lake Trail	7.5 miles	12 km
Jct. with Hoodoo Basin Trail	8.5	13.5
Bootjack Gap	12.5	20
Crandall Ranger Station	28.5	45.5

From the junction with the Lamar River Trail, the Miller Creek Trail climbs up and away from Miller Creek and continues above the creek almost the entire way to the Canoe Lake junction. The trail travels through burned forest, lodgepole pine forest, and occasional meadows. Look for elk in these meadows during the morning and evening. In the first 7 miles the trail gains only about 700 feet in elevation.

From the junction with the Canoe Lake Trail, the Miller Creek Trail descends to the shore of Miller Creek at a N.P.S. patrol cabin. (Here the Hoodoo Basin Trail veers off to the southeast across Miller Creek). From the patrol cabin the Miller Creek trail climbs moderately for about 3 miles through spruce, fir, and pine forest. It then climbs more steeply through whitebark pine for the last mile to the park boundary at 9,200' Bootjack Gap. The trail has climbed about 1500 feet in the 4 miles from the patrol cabin to the pass. From the gap there is a great view to the east of the Absaroka Range and its foothills in the Shoshone National Forest.

A U.S.F.S. trail continues into Shoshone Forest, following Papoose Creek Trail up and down for 16 miles to Crandall Ranger Station on the Sunlight Basin Road. Topographic maps are a must for this section of trail.

HOODOO BASIN TRAIL
(11 miles, 17.5 km)

The Hoodoo Basin Trail travels from the Miller Creek Trail (8.5 miles from the Lamar River Trail and 17.5 miles from the Lamar Trailhead) to the park's east boundary. Starting from the Miller Creek Trail, the Hoodoo Basin Trail immediately crosses Miller Creek. This crossing is usually calf deep after mid July. After the crossing, the trail climbs through forest and meadows to the saddle of Parker Peak at 9,600 feet. At this point you will have come 4.5 miles from Miller Creek and climbed 2,100 vertical feet. The view of the Lamar area and the Mirror Plateau is superb, but don't get so caught up in the scenery that you forget about grizzlies. They feed in these high meadows all through the summer.

Upon leaving the Parker Peak saddle, the trail descends into the Hoodoo Basin, named for its weirdly shaped volcanic rock formations. After descending about 400 feet, the trail climbs back up about 500 feet to open meadows where elk and grizzly bear are occasionally spotted. The trail again descends about 200 feet into another valley, then climbs back out to the park's east boundary. From this point the trail climbs steadily as it parallels the boundary through picturesque meadows for 3 miles. It's hard to surpass the view available from these meadows; high peaks, open ridge tops, and forested valleys surround you. The Hoodoo Basin Trail ends when it again joins the park boundary at 10,470 feet. It's possible to continue on a Forest Service trail down to Sunlight Creek and the Sunlight Basin Road in Shoshone National Forest. Topographic maps of Sunlight Peak and Dead Indian Peak should be consulted for hikes in this area. *Map 8*

CANOE LAKE TRAIL
(4 miles, 6.5 km)

The Canoe Lake Trail starts from the Miller Creek Trail (7.5 miles from the Lamar River Trail and 16.5 miles from the Lamar Trailhead) and climbs up to Canoe Lake and the park's east boundary. Parts of this trail were burned in the fires of 1988. The trail climbs about 1,900 feet, mainly through forest, to the meadows surrounding Canoe Lake. These meadows attract both bear and bison, and are actually along one of the bison's main routes of summer movement. If you're fortunate enough to catch a glimpse of these huge, shaggy beasts sprinting along a high alpine ridge, it's guaranteed to be a sight you won't soon forget. The park boundary is just a short ways above Canoe Lake. A Forest Service Trail descends from the park boundary down to Timber Creek and out to Crandall Creek Ranger Station (approx. 17.5 miles from Canoe Lake) which is reached from the Sunlight Basin Road in the Shoshone National Forest. Ernest Hemingway visited, and wrote about, the Timber Creek and Crandall Creek areas during the 1930's. He obviously loved the place and longingly described the mountains, grizzlies, elk, and bighorn sheep in an article for the February 1939 issue of Vogue, called "The Clark's Fork Valley, Wyoming." It's refreshing to see how his descriptions remain accurate today. In his understated style, Ernie was right; it's "good country." *Map 8*

FROST LAKE TRAIL
(5.5 miles, 9 km)

The Frost Lake Trail travels from Cold Creek Junction on the Lamar River Trail (16 miles from the Lamar Trailhead) to the park's east boundary near Frost Lake. A portion of this trail is relatively new and thus won't be shown on maps put out before 1980. Much of the forest along this trail was burned to various degrees by the fires of 1988. From Cold Creek Junction the Frost Lake Trail immediately crosses the Lamar River, which is knee deep to thigh deep after mid July and always slippery. Once on the south side of the river, the trail parallels the river for about 1 mile upstream, mainly through meadows. It then begins to climb steeply up to a broad ridge through burned forest. The trail now follows the ridge as it climbs moderately at first, and then steeply, through whitebark pine to an open plateau on the park's east boundary. From this plateau there is a superb view of Castor Peak and Little Saddle and Saddle Mountains. There is no marked trail to Frost Lake, but it isn't difficult to find with a compass and a topographic map.

From the east boundary there is a very scenic 13 mile Forest Service trail that travels through the Absaroka Wilderness Area of the Shoshone National Forest. This trail descends to the North Fork of the Shoshone River and comes out to "civilization" at Pahaska Tepee on the Cody Highway, 2 miles east of Yellowstone's East Entrance Station. *Map 8*

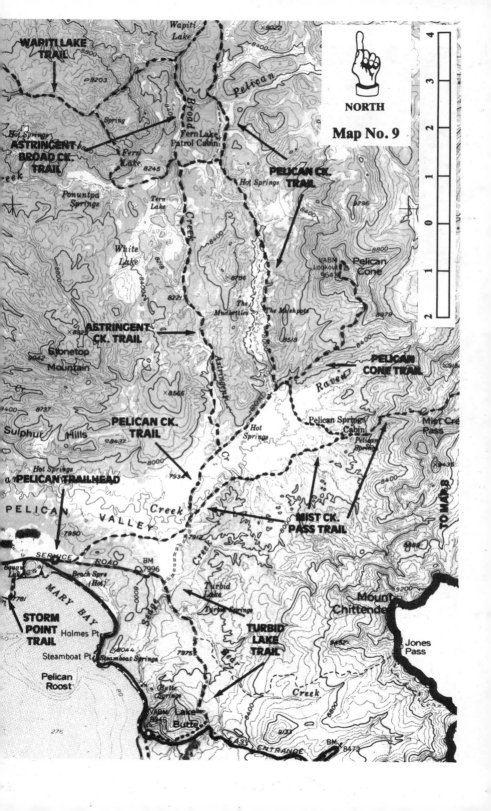

Bull elk near Turbid Lake.

PELICAN VALLEY AREA

This section of the backcountry includes Pelican Valley and the headwaters of Pelican and Broad Creeks. The trails here reach out over Pelican Valley, to backcountry lakes and thermal features, to the top of Pelican Cone, and over Mist Creek Pass to the Lamar Area.

While Pelican Valley proper is a wide open meadow, most of the rest of the area is forested. Much of this forest was burned in the fires of 1988 and some was burned in the fires of 1981. Overnight camping is allowed at designated campsites outside of Pelican Valley.

Bear Management in Pelican Valley

Pelican Valley has been the focus of some major grizzly bear management programs in the past few years. In the early 1980's the National Park Service kept Pelican Valley closed to human use until July 4. This allowed grizzly bears undisturbed use of the valley during critical spring feeding months. In August 1984, Pelican Valley was closed for a month after a woman was killed by a grizzly bear at nearby White Lake. During the ensuing investigation, and from sightings gathered by Pelican Cone Lookout Kerry Gunther, it was confirmed that many grizzly bears were using the area throughout the summer. Since that time, overnight camping by hikers in Pelican Valley proper has not been allowed. Pelican Valley was made a day-use-only area, and hiking was allowed only between the hours of 9 AM and 7PM. Kerry Gunther spent several summers on Pelican Cone using a telescope to scan Pelican Valley from sunrise to sundown, watching for bears and recording their movements. Gunther's observations seem to show a correlation between human activity and bear activity. Put simply, as human activity increased, bear activity decreased—and vice versa.

Researchers have deemed Pelican Valley some of the best grizzly bear habitat in Yellowstone. It's not unusual for hikers to see grizzlies here; and between 1985 and 1989 there were a few people that saw bears more closely than is desirable. A few were treed by bears and one person mauled. These attacks apparently all involved a sow with cubs. Because of this frequent bear activity, Pelican Valley may often be completely closed for short periods due to encounters between people and bears. The daily restricted hours (7PM to 9AM) are still in effect as of this writing, and have been strictly enforced in the past. Those found violating the closure have been fined. Because of these restrictions and the lack of people during the morning and evening, the bears are allowed a few hours each day to leave the security of the trees and venture out into the valley to feed. Early in the season before Pelican Valley opens for use, Gunther has observed the bears wandering freely through the open meadows, feeding on winterkill carcasses, grazing, and even chasing and catching elk—in other words, behaving as if the place belonged to them. Allowing the bears this de facto preserve requires some compromises from the hikers; and most have made these compromises gladly.

PELICAN CREEK TRAIL

The Pelican Creek Trail starts from the Pelican Valley Trailhead which is located on a spur road just north of Indian Pond, 3.5 miles east of Fishing Bridge Junction. The trail takes you through diverse scenery as it follows Pelican Creek from the open grassy meadows of Pelican Valley, past mud pots and hot springs, and through the lodgepole pine forests to Wapiti Lake. This entire area receives a great deal of bear use, so be alert. *Map 9*

From Pelican Valley trailhead to:

Pelican Creek Bridge	3.3 miles	5.3 km
Junction with Astringent Creek Trail	5	8
Pelican Creek ford	6.5	10.5
Mud Pot	11.5	18.5
Cutoff Trail to Broad Creek	12.5	20
Wapiti Lake	16.5	26.5

For the first ¼ mile the Pelican Creek Trail follows the old Turbid Lake Road and then veers off north through meadows towards Pelican Valley. Once in the valley there will be good views of the Absaroka Range, meandering Pelican Creek, and probably some lone bison. After crossing Pelican Creek by bridge, the trail continues through open meadows, over two small creeks, past Astringent Creek Trail Junction, and back to Pelican Creek.

After fording Pelican Creek (knee deep in early July), the trail comes to a junction. (To the right is the trail leading to the Pelican Cone Trail, Pelican Springs Patrol Cabin, and Mist Creek Pass. This trail also can be used to loop back to the Pelican Valley Trailhead). The Pelican Creek Trail veers uphill to the left (north) and then parallels Pelican Creek for the next 3 miles. In this section the trail passes a small thermal area containing some mud pots and fumaroles, and goes through meadows containing a wide variety of wildflowers. The trail crosses Pelican Creek in an open meadow, follows the creek on the west for about a mile then crosses it again. After crossing the creek, the trail enters the forest and soon comes to an impressive mud pot, which is off the trail to the east.

At the junction with the cutoff trail to Broad Creek, the Pelican Creek Trail continues north. (The cutoff trail heads west across Pelican Creek). After passing Fern Lake Patrol Cabin, and crossing Pelican Creek a final time, the Pelican Creek Trail heads into the forest and ends at Wapiti Lake. There are well used bison trails veering off in this area so make certain the trail you follow is marked with orange markers. Wapiti Lake is surrounded by forest, and is home to waterfowl during the summer. It is not very scenic and it contains no fish. The best thing that can be said for it is that it's very remote.

PELICAN CONE TRAIL
(4 miles, 6.5 kilometers)

The shortest route to Pelican Cone starts at Pelican Valley Trailhead and follows the Pelican Creek Trail for 6.5 miles to the Pelican Creek ford. From the north side of the creek the Pelican Cone Trail angles right. After about ¼ mile, it then turns uphill into the trees. (The trail to Pelican Springs Cabin continues southeast across Raven Creek). The trail climbs through forest the entire way, gaining about 1600 feet in the 4 miles to the top. There are no sources of drinking water along this last 4 miles, other than a snowfield on the summit. The far reaching view from the top includes the Teton Range and Yellowstone Lake to the south, Mt. Washburn to the northwest and the skyline of the Absaroka Range to the east. There is a fire lookout on the summit that is occasionally manned (or womanned, as the case may be.) *Map 9*

ASTRINGENT CREEK/BROAD CREEK TRAIL

This trail travels from the Pelican Valley Trailhead to Wapiti Lake by way of Astringent Creek and Broad Creek. The entire trail is fairly level and offers no long ranging vistas, as it is mainly down in the forest. White Lake, Tern Lake, and Fern Lake are all passed on the way. These lakes and their meadows are good spots for viewing wildlife. Swans, Canada geese, a wide variety of ducks, great blue herons, sandhill cranes, and bald eagles are all seen here along with moose and elk. Bears are also present, but not seen as frequently. Much of this area has been burned by natural fires during the 1980's and presents a real mosaic of burn and regrowth. Mosquitoes can be quite numerous on the upper portions of this trail. Because you must travel through Pelican Valley to gain access to this trail, check at a ranger station for any hiking restrictions before you leave.

Pelican Valley Trailhead (on spur road 3.5 miles east of Fishing Bridge Jct.) to:

Astringent Creek Trail	5 miles	8 km
White Lake	9	14.5
Tern Lake	10	16
Jct. with cutoff trail to Pelican Creek	11.5	18.5
Fern Lake Trail	12	19.2
Wapiti Lake	16	25.5

To reach the start of the Astringent Creek/Broad Creek Trail you must follow the Pelican Creek Trail for 5 miles until you come to the trail junction just northeast of the crossing of Astringent Creek. After leaving the Pelican Creek Trail, the Astringent Creek/Broad Creek Trail heads north along the meadows of Astringent Creek. There are 2 bridged crossings of Astringent Creek along this section. After 3.5 miles the trail leaves Astringent Creek and crosses a low ridge to White Lake and the drainage of Broad Creek. Only a small portion of White Lake is visible from the trail. In 1984 a Swiss woman was attacked and killed by a grizzly bear while camped in this area.

At 11.5 miles you'll meet the cutoff trail to the upper Pelican Creek Trail (1 mile away to the east). From this junction the Astringent/Broad Creek Trail enters the forest and soon comes to another trail junction. (Here, the Fern Lake Trail heads west, across Broad Creek, to Fern Lake, ½ mile away, and Ponuntpa Hot Springs, 1.5 miles away and an occasional wintering spot for bison. The Fern Lake Trail eventually joins the Wapiti Lake Trail and can be followed back to Canyon Village). The Astringent/-Broad Creek Trail continues to follow Broad Creek through meadows and forest to the junction with the Wapiti Lake Trail. To reach Wapiti Lake turn right (east) and follow this trail as it climbs about 300 feet in the ½ mile to the lake. From Wapiti Lake you may loop back to Pelican Valley by way of the Pelican Creek Trail. *Map 9*

MIST CREEK PASS TRAIL

This trail travels from the Pelican Valley Trailhead over Mist Creek Pass to The Lamar River Trail. The highlight of the trail is the section through Pelican Valley. Here you may see moose wading in the creek, osprey diving for trout, trout rising for an insect hatch, an eagle or sandhill cranes soaring overhead, big bull bison grazing on a hillside or a grizzly bear loping along the edge of the forest. Don't count on seeing all this in one day; but don't be surprised if you do. Much of the forest along this route was burned during the fires of 1988. *Maps 8, 9*

From Pelican Valley Trailhead (on spur road 3.5 miles east of Fishing Bridge) to:

Pelican Creek bridge	3.3 miles	5 km
Pelican Springs	7	11
Mist Creek Pass	9	14.5
Lamar River Trail	17	27
Lamar River Trailhead	33	53

From the trailhead, the trail follows the Pelican Creek Trail to the Pelican Creek Bridge. The Mist Creek Trail veers off here and continues on the east side of Pelican Creek. This section of trail is often overgrown and hard to follow through the marshy meadow. Just keep paralleling the creek and the trail will become visible again once you reach drier ground. The trail then goes over rolling hills and across small streams; one of which may have to be waded. At Pelican Springs Patrol Cabin there is another junction. (The trail to Pelican Cone goes left, west, here). The Mist Creek Pass Trail goes straight ahead, northeast. After climbing about 600 feet through 2 miles of burned forest you will arrive at Mist Creek Pass. The trail descends to Mist Creek Meadows, where there are some pretty campsites; and where elk are occasionally seen early and late in the day. From the meadows the trail descends gradually through burned forest to the meadows of the Lamar River. Here you must cross the Lamar River, which is knee deep after late July, to gain the Lamar River Trail on the river's east side. The Lamar River Trailhead (on the Northeast Entrance Road) is 16 miles away.

TURBID LAKE TRAIL
(3 miles, 5 kilometers)

This trail is actually an old dirt road which runs from Pelican Valley Trailhead to Turbid Lake, and eventually joins the East Entrance Road about 10 miles east of Fishing Bridge Junction. The directions are easy; just start at the trailhead and follow the old road east until you reach Turbid Lake. You'll pass through two large meadows on the way. Bison, elk, and bears are sometimes seen in these meadows. Most of the trail is in the forest. Turbid Lake shows the effects of the thermal features underneath it's surface. Its water is discolored and bubbling from released gases. Not a picturesque area, but interesting. There is a great deal of bear activity in this area, and a man was mauled by a grizzly here in 1986.

From Turbid Lake it's possible to follow the old road south through thick forest for another 3 miles to where a trail veers off to the west (this trail leads to 9 Mile Trailhead, 9 miles east of Fishing Bridge Junction on the East Entrance Road). If you stay on the old road you'll reach the East Entrance Road in about ¼ mile. There is no trailhead or parking area here. *Maps 9, 22*

STORM POINT TRAIL
(1.5 miles, 3 km)

This is a good short trail down to the shoreline of Yellowstone Lake. Unfortunately, the trail is frequently closed due to grizzly bear activity. Check at Lake Ranger Station or Fishing Bridge Visitor Center before leaving for the trailhead. The trail starts at the Indian Pond parking area, 3.5 miles east of Fishing Bridge and directly across from the Pelican Valley Trailhead. The trail travels through open meadows above Indian Pond, where Goldeneye ducks, Canada geese, and even occasional loons can be seen. Be certain to give a wide berth to the big bull bison which frequently graze in these meadows. Once down near the lake, the trail veers to the right and heads into the trees. The trail stays in the trees until it reaches the tip of Storm Point, which is a windy viewpoint of Yellowstone Lake. Prominent are Stevenson Island and the massive Mt. Sheridan to the south. *Map 9*

HOWARD EATON TRAIL—FISHING BRIDGE TO CANYON

The Howard Eaton Trail travels from Fishing Bridge to the Grand Canyon of the Yellowstone. It is part of the old Howard Eaton Trail system that follows the route of the present day Grand Loop Road. Much of this trail travels through Hayden Valley, which is some of the park's best wildlife habitat. Unfortunately most of this stretch of trail is also within sight and sound of the main road. The first couple miles of the north and south end of the trail are probably the most worthwhile sections to hike, as they both offer interesting terrain away from the highway. *Map 12*

From Fishing Bridge Trailhead to:

LeHardy Rapids	3 miles	4.8 km
Buffalo Ford	5	8
Sour Creek	11	17.6
Wrangler Lake Trail	12	19.2
South Rim Drive Trailhead	14	22.4

The trail begins about 400 yards behind (north of) the Fishing Bridge Store and follows a barricaded service road. The Howard Eaton Trail veers left off this service road after about ¼ mile. The first mile of trail travels through open meadows where a variety of wildlife, including bears may be encountered. The Yellowstone River is nearby and offers an excellent spot to view waterfowl such as white pelicans, swans, and goldeneye ducks. Continuing north through forest, you'll reach a good overlook of LeHardy Rapids. Further north, the trail passes Buffalo Ford, which was used by the Nez Perce Indians in their escape from the U.S. Cavalry in 1877. The trail then passes by some riverside thermal features as it passes opposite the Mud Volcano Area. Most of the rest of the trail is through the open meadows of Hayden Valley. This stretch of trail can be hot and dry during the summer.

Just south of Sour Creek, you'll come to a trail junction that may or may not be marked. The right fork leads to junctions with the Wrangler Lake Trail and the Clear Lake Trail and eventually to the Chittenden Bridge Trailhead. The Howard Eaton Trail veers to the left (west) and crosses Sour Creek, which is an easy knee deep crossing after mid July. The trail then continues through the meadows of Hayden Valley and along the edge of the forest until it arrives at the Chittenden Bridge Trailhead (on the South Rim Drive—first right turn after the bridge over the Yellowstone River).

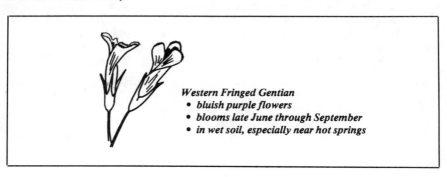

Western Fringed Gentian
- *bluish purple flowers*
- *blooms late June through September*
- *in wet soil, especially near hot springs*

CANYON AREA

Although the Grand Canyon of the Yellowstone is the main point of interest in the Canyon Area, it really doesn't receive a very extensive coverage by true "backcountry" trails. Yet there are many short walkways that lead up to, around, and in to this spectacular canyon. These walkways are described in a leaflet that also explains the area's interesting geology and which is available from the Canyon Village Visitor Center. The only backcountry trails that offer good views of the canyon are the Point Sublime Trail, the Glacial Boulder Trail, and the Seven Mile Hole Trail. The remaining trails in the Canyon area take you through a variety of terrain, from forested lakes to large open meadows and even to the top of Mt. Washburn. Grizzly bears inhabit much of the area, and elk, moose, and bison are all frequently seen.

CLEAR LAKE/RIBBON LAKE LOOP TRAIL

The Clear Lake/Ribbon Lake Loop Trail is an easy, relatively level, 6 mile trail that offers the opportunity to see a variety of wildflowers, an occasional moose or even grizzly bear, and some charming backcountry lakes. *Map 10*

From Chittenden Bridge Trailhead to:

Clear Lake	1.5 miles	2.5 km
Lillypad Lake	2	3
Ribbon Lake	3	5
Jct. with Wapiti Lake Trail	3.5	6
Chittenden Trailhead	6	10

This trail starts at the Chittenden Bridge Trailhead. To reach this trailhead, turn on to the South Rim Drive to Artist Point (approx. 2 miles south of Canyon on the Canyon-Lake Road), You will immediately cross the Chittenden Bridge over the Yellowstone River. Now make the first right turn after the bridge. This parking area is the Chittenden Trailhead.

From the trailhead the trail climbs an open, grassy hillside and then descends to a trail junction. Turn north at this junction and you will reach Clear Lake in about ½ mile. The trail skirts the east shoreline of this lovely hot spring-fed lake and then continues through meadows and forest to Lillypad Lake. From Lillypad Lake, the trail climbs a forested ridge and then descends to Ribbon Lake and an unnamed lake to the east. From Ribbon Lake a spur trail veers north to Silver Cord Cascade which is a small stream that tumbles about 1,000 feet down the side of the Grand Canyon. From Ribbon Lake the Clear Lake/Ribbon Lake Trail turns west and descends through forest past a small lake to the Sour Creek Trail junction. The trail then climbs up the open grassy hillside and returns to the Chittenden Trailhead.

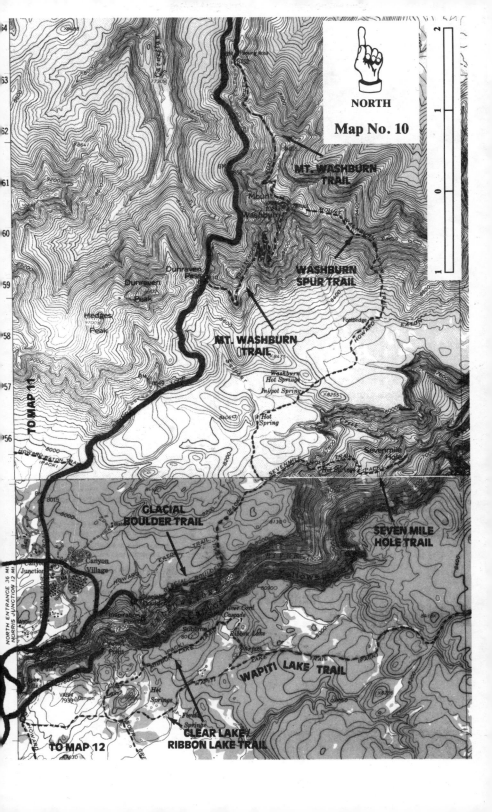

NORTH

Map No. 10

MT. WASHBURN
TRAIL

WASHBURN
SPUR TRAIL

MT. WASHBURN
TRAIL

GLACIAL
BOULDER TRAIL

SEVEN MILE
HOLE TRAIL

WAPITI LAKE TRAIL

CLEAR LAKE/
RIBBON LAKE TRAIL

TO MAP 11

TO MAP 12

NORTH ENTRANCE 36 MI.
NORRIS JUNCTION 12 MI.

Dunraven Peak

Dunraven Pass

Dunraven
Peak

Hedges
Peak

Mount
Washburn

Washburn
Hot Springs

Inkpot Spring

Hot
Spring

Sevenmile
Hole

Footbridge

Canyon
Junction

Canyon
Village

Inspiration
Point

Sublime
Cascade

Ribbon Lake

Clear
Lake

Hot
Springs

Bighorn Rams

MT. WASHBURN TRAILS

Dunraven Pass Picnic Area to		
Mt. Washburn Lookout	3 miles	5 km
Chittenden Road Parking Area to		
Mt. Washburn Lookout	3	5

If you have time to take but one short hike in Yellowstone, make it Mt. Washburn. During the summer wildflowers and bighorn sheep abound on the mountain's slopes. The bighorns migrate from their lowland winter range to this high spot to spend the summer. They seem to accept the presence of hikers and often feed surprisingly close to the trail. They are not visible from the trail everyday, but when they do make an appearance Kodak profits for the day take a turn for the better. The price of film becomes no object as people point and shoot with reckless abandon. Nowhere else in Yellowstone can amateur photographers get such close-ups of bighorn with their instant cameras. Ravens, marmots, and golden-mantled ground squirrels are also frequently seen here. The view from the summit of Mt. Washburn is tremendous; it will seem as if the whole park is below you. With the help of your map you'll be able to spot the Grand Canyon, Yellowstone Lake, the Teton Range, Hayden Valley, Electric Peak and maybe even some steam rising from the geyser basins along the Firehole River.

Both trails start from the Canyon-Tower Road, the southern trail starts at Dunraven Pass Picnic Area, the northern trail at the Chittenden Road Parking Area. Both of the trails to the summit are 3 miles in length and both climb about 1,400 feet. The hiking isn't steep, but it is steady, and it's not difficult if taken at a slow pace. Because Mt. Washburn is over 10,000 feet high, it doesn't take much for the weather to turn uncomfortable. Even though it may be warm at the trailhead, count on it being colder and much windier near the top. Summer storms are not unusual on Mt. Washburn, so be certain to include some rain gear in your pack. Once you make it to the summit you'll be able to get out of the wind in the day-use shelter for hikers that's located on the bottom floor of the lookout tower.

In recent years there have been a few points of misunderstanding about the Mt. Washburn hike that will hopefully be clarified here.

—From the south, the Mt. Washburn Trail starts at Dunraven Pass Picnic Area, and not at the Dunraven Road Picnic Area a few miles away.

—Due to heavy use of this area, the delicate alpine vegetation is being severely trampled and numerous false trails have been started. Please help reduce this source of visual, as well as physical, impact by staying on the old road that serves as the main trail.

—Don't feed the bighorn sheep. As explained earlier, feeding does not benefit the sheep and the sight of a bighorn with a pickle in it's mouth certainly is not what most people hike up Mt. Washburn to see. *Map 10*

MT. WASHBURN SPUR TRAIL

From Glacial Boulder Trailhead (on Inspiration Point Road) to:

Jct. with Howard Eaton Trail	2 miles	3 km
Jct. with 7-Mile Hole Trail	3	5
Washburn Hot Springs	4.8	7.7
Washburn Spur Trail	6	9.5
Summit of Mt. Washburn	8.5	13.5
Dunraven Pass Picnic Area	11.5	18.5

To reach the Mt. Washburn Spur Trail, start at the Glacial Boulder Trailhead on the road to Inspiration Point. Follow the Glacial Boulder Trail until it meets the Howard Eaton Trail; then follow the Howard Eaton Trail northeast towards Tower. Continue on the Howard Eaton Trail past the turnoff for the Seven Mile Hole Trail. At Washburn Hot Springs you will find some interesting thermal features, including mud pots. The Howard Eaton Trail continues through a large meadow, where there is a good view of Mt. Washburn above and wildflowers below, and on to the junction with the Mt. Washburn Spur Trail. (The Howard Eaton Trail continues towards Tower, but is closed most of the year due to a Bear Management Area further north). From this point the Mt. Washburn spur trail climbs about 2,000 feet in the 2.5 miles to the top. There are very good views to the south most of the way up, and especially when you reach the top of Washburn's East Ridge. Grizzly bears frequent this area; so stay alert.

The Washburn Spur Trail is the most difficult and least traveled of the 3 trails up Mt. Washburn. An enjoyable way to hike this trail is to take the trail from Dunraven Pass up to the summit of Mt. Washburn and then hike the Washburn Spur Trail down to Canyon Village. Due to the steepness of this trail, it's much easier to enjoy the spectacular view while strolling downhill than while puffing uphill. *Map 10*

WRANGLER LAKE TRAIL
(3 miles, 4.8 kilometers)

The Wrangler Lake Trail starts at the Chittenden Bridge Trailhead on the road to Artist Point. Follow the Clear Lake/Ribbon Lake Loop Trail as it climbs through open meadows where bison are often seen. After approximately ¾ mile, the trail to Clear Lake will veer off to the left near the top of a hill. Follow the right fork of the trail up, over, and down a hill and then up another. The trail to Wrangler Lake veers off to the right in the clump of trees at the top of this hill. For the next ½ mile the Wrangler Lake Trail then goes down through lodgepole pine forest and grassy meadows and over a small warm stream to another junction. Wrangler Lake Trail turns east through sage meadows to Sour Creek, where it makes two knee deep crossings of this slow moving creek and its tributary. Once across the creek the trail heads south through the woods to Wrangler Lake. The lake is almost completely surrounded by trees and its shoreline is quite marshy. As you might guess, mosquitoes can be a real problem here. *Map 10*

WAPITI LAKE TRAIL
(15.5 miles, 25 km)

The Wapiti Lake Trail travels from the Chittenden Bridge Trailhead through stands of pine, spruce and fir to Broad Creek and Wapiti Lake. This hike is for lovers of remote dense forest. Far-ranging panoramic views are not a part of the scenery for the majority of this trail.

The Wapiti Lake Trail starts out through open meadows that often hold elk and occasionally a bear. The trail then climbs gradually through the forest for 12 miles to a wooded pass at 9,000 feet. The trail descends steeply to the meadows of Broad Creek where elk and moose are seen during the summer. The meadows of Broad Creek can be mucky and are certain to filled with mosquitoes during July. After an easy crossing of Broad Creek, the trail climbs about 300 feet through forest to the tree lined shores of Wapiti Lake. *Map 10*

GLACIAL BOULDER TRAIL
(2 miles, 3 km)

The Glacial Boulder trail provides a good view of the Grand Canyon of the Yellowstone, although not quite as good as the views from Inspiration Point (which you can drive to). The trail also provides access to the Howard Eaton Trail and Seven Mile Hole Trail. There are some short stretches of steep up and downhill, but the trail is generally level as it parallels the canyon rim for most of its 2 miles. It is also out of sight of the view into the canyon much of the way.

The trail starts at Glacial Boulder which is about 2 miles from Canyon Village on the road to Inspiration Point (which is off the North Rim Drive). The Glacial Boulder is a 500 ton hunk of 600 million year old gneiss sitting on top of 600 thousand year old rhyolite. The older rock is sitting on top of the younger due to a glacier picking up the old rock from a distant exposed bed of gneiss, and dumping it here about 15,000 years ago. A local custom among hikers is to try and scale the 15 foot high rock before starting out on the trail. Try it, but no fair using the trees. *Map 10*

SEVEN MILE HOLE TRAIL
(5.5 miles, 9 km)

The Seven Mile Hole Trail provides the hiker with a different type of view of the Grand Canyon. This trail takes you to the bottom of a section of the canyon that is broad, mostly forested, and very impressive. Because the trail leads to the Yellowstone River it's popular with fishermen. The Yellowstone River is the only source of water along the trail, so be certain to bring plenty of water with you. If you do drink from the Yellowstone River, it would be foolish not to treat your water.

The trail follows Glacial Boulder Trail along the rim of the canyon, through lodgepole pine forest, for the first 2 miles. It then joins with the Howard Eaton Trail for the next mile. The Seven Mile Hole Trail then leaves the Howard Eaton Trail and soon begins the descent into the canyon. The trail drops about 1,400 feet in 1.5 miles, sections of which are fairly steep. Take it easy on the descent and save your leg muscles for the climb back out. The old cliche about this trail, "5 miles in and 35 out," can feel very accurate. The descent takes you by some dormant, and some active, hot springs. Once down at the river look for ouzels fluttering around the rocks and osprey soaring overhead. *Map 10*

GREBE LAKE TRAIL
(3 mile, 5 kilometers)

Grebe Lake and Wolf Lake make up the headwaters of the Gibbon River, the start of one of the longest waterways in the world. The Gibbon flows into the Madison River, which flows into the Missouri River, which flows into the Mississippi River. So when the water from Grebe Lake finally mingles with the salt water of the Gulf of Mexico, it's travelled over 3,500 miles.

Grebe Lake's waters are home for the arctic grayling, a rare native fish of Yellowstone. This is one of the few spots left in the country, outside of Alaska, that has a viable population of these beautiful fish. Grebe Lake is also a summer home for a variety of waterfowl. Ducks, loons, California gulls, and trumpeter swans are all seen here. The lake is almost completely surrounded by meadows that are growing spots for a number of summer wildflowers. These meadow are usually damp throughout the summer which means you may encounter numerous mosquitoes, at least until early August. Luckily there's usually an afternoon breeze blowing across the lake that keeps the bugs at bay until evening. Grizzly bears are sometimes seen in this area during early summer, so be certain to check at Canyon Visitor Center for the latest in bear information. Moose and deer are also seen throughout the summer at dawn and dusk.

The Grebe Lake Trail starts from Grebe Lake Trailhead, which is approximately 4 miles west of Canyon on the Canyon-Norris Road. This trail, which follows an old fire road almost the entire way, is the shortest and driest route into Grebe Lake. The first mile of the trail winds through meadows near the edge of a forest. The remainder of the trail winds through a dense lodgepole pine forest that was heavily burned during the fires of 1988. Once at the lake, the trail follows the shoreline, through meadows, to the east. Here it meets the Howard Eaton Trail. By following the Howard Eaton Trail west you can travel to Wolf Lake (2 miles away), Ice Lake, and Norris Campground. By taking the Howard Eaton Trail to the east you can go to Cascade Lake (2 miles away) and Canyon Village. *Map 11*

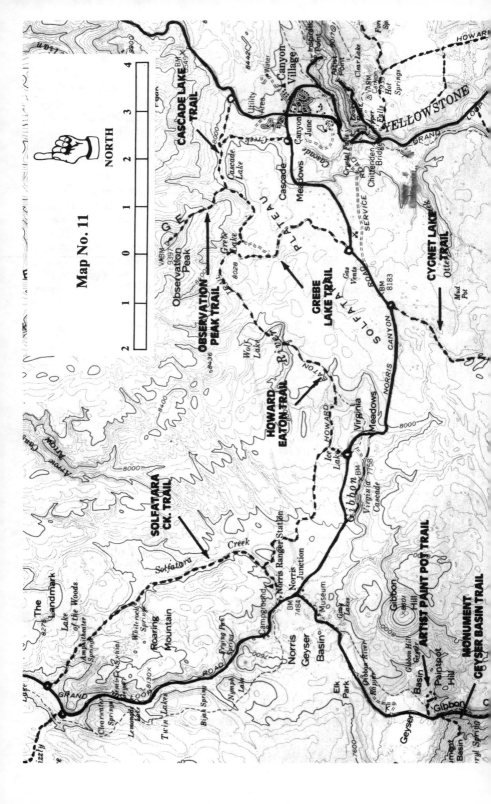

TRAILS TO CASCADE LAKE

Cascade Lake is a small lake sitting at the base of the Washburn Range. Cascade Creek flows out of the lake and through grassy meadows and stands of willows. The willows provide food and building materials for beaver. In years past there has been a beaver lodge on the south shore of Cascade Lake and a lodge and dam on Cascade Creek. Cascade Lake and its meadows are also home to numerous waterfowl, otter, coyotes, moose, and bears. Much of this area was burned during the fires of 1988. *Map 11*

Cascade Lake Trail Picnic Area on Canyon-Tower Road to Cascade Lake	2.2 miles	3.5 km
Cascade Creek Trailhead on Canyon-Norris road to Cascade Lake	2.5	4

There are 2 short trails to Cascade Lake. The shortest and most enjoyable is the trail that starts at the Cascade Lake Trail Picnic Area (1.5 miles north of Canyon Jct. on the Canyon-Tower Road). This trail starts at the west side of the picnic area and soon brings you out through open meadows and over small spring creeks. The wildflower display here can be quite spectacular during mid summer. After approximately 1.2 miles, this trail joins the Cascade Creek Trail and continues on to Cascade Lake. Total distance is 2.2 miles.

The Cascade Creek Trail starts at Cascade Creek Trailhead (about ½ mile west of Canyon Jct. on the Canyon-Norris Road). This trail follows Cascade Creek through burned forest to Cascade Lake. The disadvantage to this trail is that it is used by the large and frequent commercial horse rides to Cascade Lake. If you hike the trail during, or soon after, one of these trips, the smell of horse urine and manure can add a less-than-pleasant sensory aspect to your hike. The advantage to this trail is that the trailhead is an easy walk from Canyon Village. Total distance of this trail is 2.5 miles.

OBSERVATION PEAK TRAIL
(3 miles, 5 kilometers)

The trail to Observation Peak climbs about 1,400 feet in three miles. Although it's not shown on pre 1980 maps, the trail provides a very nice view of Grebe Lake, Hayden Valley and the Central Plateau. The Observation Peak Trail starts at the northwest corner of Cascade Lake. This can be reached by any of the three trails to Cascade Lake, the shortest of which is 2.2 miles. The trail travels mainly through open meadows and whitebark pine forest. *Map 11*

HOWARD EATON TRAIL—TO ICE LAKE, WOLF LAKE, and GREBE LAKE

The Howard Eaton Trail actually travels from Norris to Canyon but this description will deal just with the section from Ice Lake to Grebe Lake. The other sections of the Howard Eaton Trail are covered in the Norris Campground-Ice Lake Trail and the Trails to Cascade Lake descriptions.

This whole area is a part of the Solfatara Plateau, which sits at about 8,000 feet above sea level. This plateau is a relatively flat lodgepole pine forest, much of which was burned in the fires of 1988. Ice Lake is penned in by this forest, while Wolf Lake is surrounded by open marshy meadows. Wolf Lake is home for a variety of waterfowl. Sandhill cranes and herons have been spotted here especially along the lake's shoreline away from the trail. Moose may also be seen in this area. As in Grebe Lake, grayling and rainbow trout inhabit the waters of Wolf Lake.

Ice Lake Trailhead (3.5 miles east of Norris on the Norris Canyon Road) to:

Ice Lake	0.3 miles	0.5 km
Wolf Lake	4	6.5
Grebe Lake (west shore)	5	8
Cascade Lake	8	13
Cascade Creek Trailhead	10.8	17

From the Ice Lake Trailhead it's only a couple minutes easy walk to Ice Lake. Here you join the Howard Eaton Trail. (If you turn west, the trail will take you to Norris Campground). To reach Wolf Lake continue east on the Howard Eaton Trail along Ice Lake's north shore. From Ice Lake the trail climbs gently through lodgepole pine forest to the meadows of Wolf Lake. There are two easy crossings of the Gibbon River in this section of trail. Here the Gibbon resembles a creek more than a river. There are two more easy crossings in the meadow east of Wolf Lake.

From Wolf Lake the trail continues east through meadow and forest to the west shore of Grebe Lake. The Howard Eaton Trail continues around the north shore of Grebe Lake until it meets the junction with the Grebe Lake Trail. To reach Cascade Lake, stay on the Howard Eaton Trail as it continues east through marshy meadows. From Cascade Lake you will be an easy 2.5 mile walk away from one of two trailheads. *Map 11*

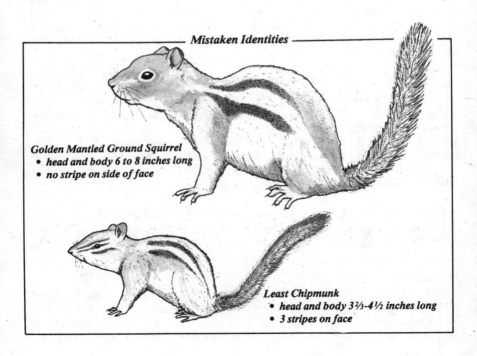

Mistaken Identities

Golden Mantled Ground Squirrel
- *head and body 6 to 8 inches long*
- *no stripe on side of face*

Least Chipmunk
- *head and body 3⅓-4½ inches long*
- *3 stripes on face*

NORRIS AREA

The main point of interest in the Norris Area is the Norris Geyser Basin, the hottest and most changeable basin in the park. The basin is covered by a network of short trails and walkways that take you past an amazing variety of thermal features. A description of these walkways and an explanation of the features are covered in a leaflet available at the Norris Geyser Basin Museum.

As for the backcountry trails, the Solfatara Creek Trail and the Ice Lake Trail start at the Norris Campground, making them convenient hikes for campers in the area. The other two trails, Monument Geyser Basin Trail and the Artist Paint Pot Trail both provide an interesting look at the off-the-beaten-track thermal areas.

SOLFATARA CREEK TRAIL

From Norris Campground to:

Whiterock Spring	3.5 miles	5.5 km
Mammoth-Norris Road (¾ mile south of Beaver Lake Picnic Area)	6.5	10

From the Norris Campground, the trail travels through the forest paralleling Solfatara Creek. (The trail to Ice Lake forks east after ¾ mile). During the summer the meadows along Solfatara Creek are an excellent place to spot elk, as well as a variety of wildflowers such as Indian paintbrush, glacial lilies, wild strawberries (fruit in late July) and sticky geraniums. Once past Whiterock Springs, the trail begins to climb gradually up to Lake of the Woods (which is actually a few hundred yards north of the trail). The trail then descends, about 400 feet in a mile, and passes by Amphitheater Springs and Lemonade Creek. There is often a bright emerald-green algae growing in Lemonade Creek, which makes the creek look much more like limeade than lemonade. Either way, don't drink the water as the sulfur springs feeding this little creek give the water a taste unlike either of the aforementioned beverages. This trail ends at a short service road off the Mammoth-Norris Road. *Map 11*

NORRIS CAMPGROUND TO ICE LAKE

From Norris Campground to:

Ice Lake	4.5 miles	7 km
Wolf Lake	8.5	14
Grebe Lake	9.5	15
Cascade Creek Trailhead	15	24

From Norris Campground, the trail to Ice Lake begins by paralleling Solfatara Creek for about ¾ mile. The Ice Lake trail then veers east, crosses the creek, and continues through the intermittently burned forest to a large meadow. This meadow often is a feeding spot for elk during summer evenings and mornings. From the meadow, the trail climbs about 300 feet in the remaining 1.5 miles to Ice Lake. Although this small lake has been stocked with over 3 million fish since 1905, it is barren of fish today. Rainbow, cutthroat trout, and grayling have all been stocked but the absence of a constantly flowing inlet and outlet stream for spawning has precluded a self sustaining fish population. The Howard Eaton Trail continues from Ice Lake to Cascade Lake, making a Norris to Canyon hike possible. Refer to the description of the Howard Eaton Trail-Ice Lake to Grebe Lake for more information. *Map 11*

MONUMENT GEYSER BASIN TRAIL
(1 mile, 1.5 km)

This short steep trail starts at the Gibbon River bridge, 5 miles south of Norris Junction on the Norris-Madison Road. The trail climbs 500 feet, mainly through lodgepole pine forest. Monument Geyser Basin has a variety of thermal features which include mud pots, sulphur pools, steam vents, and some interestingly shaped geyser cones. *Map 12*

ARTIST PAINT POT TRAIL
(0.5 mile, 0.8 km)

The trailhead for Artist Paint Pots is located about 4.5 miles south of Norris Junction, in Gibbon Meadows. This interesting little path winds through a lodgepole pine forest where harebell can be found blooming from July through mid August. The relatively level trail leads to a variety of thermal features. The main attraction among these is the mud pot located at the top of the hill where the trail begins to loop back around. This thermal area also contains some small geysers, hot pools, and steam vents. This is a very worthwhile hike. *Map 12*

CENTRAL PLATEAU AREA

The Central Plateau Area, which contains Nez Perce Valley, and Hayden Valley is an interesting spot, geologically, biologically, and historically. Geologically, the area was the center of one of the largest volcanic eruptions ever to have occurred on the face of the earth. Biologically, the area is home for two of the park's most magnificent animals, the bison and the grizzly bear. Historically, this area was used as an escape route by the Nez Perce Indians in their attempt to reach Canada in 1877.

About 2 million years ago, Yellowstone was ripped open by a powerful volcanic eruption. A huge outpouring of molten rock and ash followed, leaving a vast cavern underground where the molten rock had been before. This sudden cavern caused a huge collapse of the rocks above and left an immense crater or caldera on the surface of Yellowstone. This gigantic caldera covered over 1,000 square miles and must have been several thousand feet deep. Later volcanic flows inside the caldera have somewhat filled it; although it is still visible from a high vantage point such as Mt. Washburn. The Central Plateau is in the middle of the caldera and was formed by these later flows of molten rock. Thus the rock of the Central Plateau is volcanic, and as you'll see, lodgepole pine does very well in the volcanic soils.

At one time, Hayden Valley too was exposed volcanic rock, until it was covered by the waters of an enlarged Yellowstone Lake. This larger version of the present lake, formed by an ancient rock and ice dam, left behind sediments of silt, sand, and clay. Now because of this underlying sediment, and the resulting better quality soil, Hayden Valley is covered with grasses, sedges, and forbs instead of the lodgepole forest of the Central Plateau.

The grizzly bears and bison are both attracted to Hayden and Nez Perce Valleys because of the lush plant growth. The bison graze on the valley's vegetation in spring, summer, and fall. Come winter, many of them move to lower elevations along the Firehole River. But some stay in Nez Perce and Hayden Valleys, feeding on the valley's snow covered vegetation. The grizzly too depends on the valley's plants, especially yampa, clover, and biscuit root. The grizzly will also supplement its diet with meat, particularly during the spring. During this time bears may chase down new-born elk calves or feed on carcasses of winter killed bison. This is about the only way grizzlies ever get to eat bison steaks; they usually won't mess with an animal as huge and powerful as a live bison. Hikers could learn something from the grizzly.

In 1877, the Nez Perce Creek area was the site of a somewhat unfriendly meeting between a band of Nez Perce Indians and some early Yellowstone tourists. The Nez Perce Indians, led by Chief Joseph, had entered the park while attempting to escape the U.S. Cavalry. A radical band of the tribe attacked and captured a group of tourists that were camping in the Nez Perce Creek area. During the attack, one of the tourists, George Cowan, was shot in the head and left for dead by the Indians. As it turned out, not only did George survive and manage to escape, even after another Indian shot him in the hip, but when the bullet was finally removed from his skull, he had it made into an ornament for his watch. And if that wasn't enough excitement, Mr Cowan later had a creek in Nez Perce Valley named Cowan Creek in his honor.

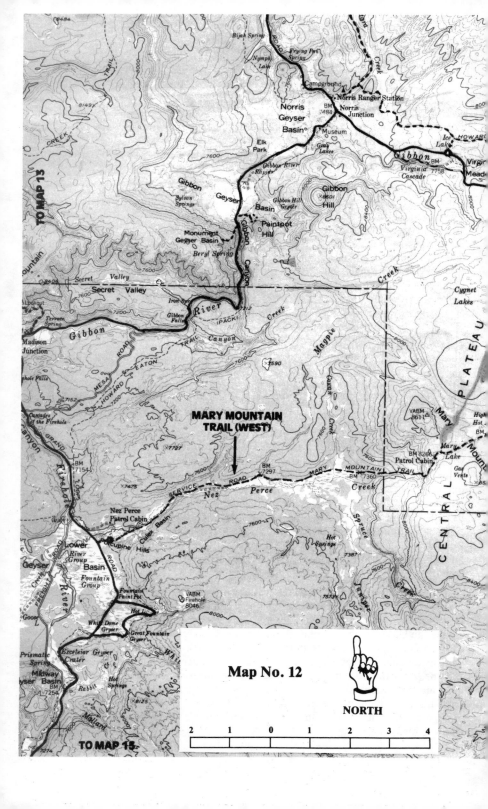

MARY MOUNTAIN
TRAIL (WEST)

Map No. 12

NORTH

2 1 0 1 2 3 4

TO MAP 15

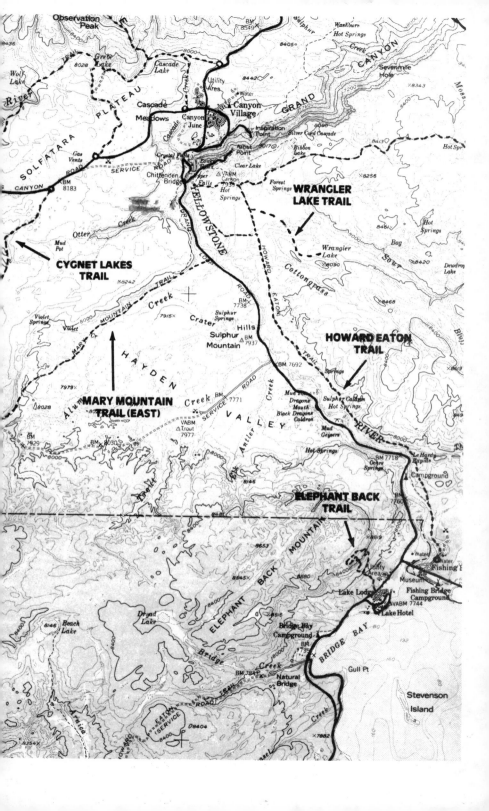

MARY MOUNTAIN TRAIL—WEST
(Also known as Nez Perce Creek Trail)

The western portion of the Mary Mountain Trail travels from the trailhead on the Madison-Old Faithful Road (about 6 miles south of Madison Jct.) to Mary Lake. The trail follows Nez Perce Creek through lodgepole pine forest and meadows most of the way. Much of the forest in this area was burned during the fires of 1988. Bison are often seen in this area during spring (late April and May), and this is an especially good time and place to view bison cows with their new born calves. Grizzlies may also be spotted in the valley during the spring months. Because of the high concentrations of grizzly bears in the surrounding area there is no overnight camping allowed along any portion of this trail. *Map 12*

From Nez Perce Trailhead to:

Nez Perce Creek bridge	2 miles	3 km
Magpie Creek	4	6.4
Mary Lake	11	18
Trailhead on Canyon-Lake Road	20	32

From the trailhead the trail follows an old road to the bridge over Nez Perce Creek. The trail continues to travel intermittently through forest and meadow to the crossings of Magpie Creek and Cowan Creek (both can be crossed on logs). Near Cowan Creek, the trail goes through some meadows that remain soggy all summer long. Once past these meadows, the trail enters a lodgepole pine forest and climbs 900 feet, very steeply in spots, to Mary Lake. Mary Lake is a tree lined lake which holds no fish, but is home to a variety of waterfowl.

Bison herd in Upper Hayden Valley. NPS Photo.

MARY MOUNTAIN TRAIL—EAST
(9 miles, 14 km)

This trail starts at a large pullout about ¼ mile north of Alum Creek on the Canyon-Lake Road (on the north end of Hayden Valley). The tread on the first two miles of trail may be hard to follow, as this trail is relatively new. The route parallels the treeline along the edge of the meadow of Hayden Valley and follows Alum Creek, until it eventually meets the older trail where the tread is more prominent. Once you find the trail, you may still want to leave it occasionally to walk closer to Alum Creek. There are small thermal areas and a variety of water birds (mallards, sandpipers, killdeer, herons, ouzels) to be seen along this intriguing stream. Don't count on Alum Creek for drinking water: one taste will tell you why. About 4 miles from the road, the trail crosses Violet Creek and begins to gain elevation as the trail makes its way to the west end of Hayden Valley. There are many bison trails in this area so be certain to follow the trail with the orange markers. Once you're out of Hayden Valley and atop the forested Central Plateau, you soon pass Highland Hot Springs and arrive at lodgepole-lined Mary Lake. Mary Lake doesn't hold any fish but there are often coots and other waterfowl swimming here.

It's not unusual for people to hike the entire Mary Mountain Trail, East and West sections (20 miles), in a day. It's a good long day hike; but actually the most interesting sections of the trail are the first 4 miles on either side. Because of the high concentrations of grizzly bears in this area there is no overnight camping allowed along any portion of this trail. *Map 12*

CYGNET LAKES TRAIL
(4 miles, 6.5 km)

The Cygnet Lakes Trail starts at a pull off on the south side of the Norris Canyon Road, approximately 5.5 miles west of Canyon Junction. The trail travels through intermittently burned forest to the expansive meadows of the Cygnet Lakes. Moose, deer, and a variety of waterfowl may be seen in these meadows. This is a day-use-only area, no overnight camping is allowed. The trail is not maintained past Cygnet Lakes. *Map 12*

ELEPHANT BACK LOOP TRAIL
(4 miles, 6.5 km)

The Elephant Back Trail climbs about 800 vertical feet from the trailhead at 7,800' to the overlook at 8,600'. The trail starts at the Elephant Back Trailhead which is approximately 1 mile south of Fishing Bridge Junction on the road between Lake Village and Fishing Bridge. The trail starts by paralleling the road south for about 50 yards and then veers up into the trees. The trail passes the old Lake Village water source pipe and then passes under the powerline. After the powerline the trail climbs steadily through lodgepole forest. Moose and deer are frequently seen in this area. About a mile from the trailhead you will come to a trail junction. Both sides lead to the top and will join at the overlook. The left path is the shortest route to the top (about 0.8 mile away). From the overlook on top there is a sweeping panorama which takes in Pelican Valley to the left, Yellowstone Lake and its islands straight in front of you, and the Absaroka Range rising above the lake as far as you can see. *Map 12*

Grizzlies on Elephant Back Trail

In recent years grizzly bears have been actively fishing in the spawning streams around Lake Village during May and June. One of these streams flows within 30 yards of the Elephant Back Trailhead. After fishing, the bears may retire up into the woods near the Elephant Back Trail to rest. Or they may use the powerline corridor to travel south to other spawning streams. Thus with all this bear activity, it's not unusual for the Elephant Back Trail to be closed early in the season.

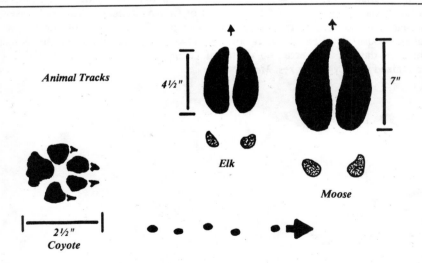

Animal Tracks

4½"

7"

Elk

Moose

2½"

Coyote

MADISON VALLEY AREA

The Madison Valley contains three trails: Harlequin Lake Trail, Purple Mountain Trail and Gneiss Creek Trail. The first two are relatively short hikes starting near the Madison Campground, while the latter is a longer hike starting about 7 miles west of the campground.

From the junction of the Firehole and Gibbon Rivers to the Gneiss Creek Trailhead, the Madison Valley is more like a canyon than a valley. Its steep walls of volcanic rock rise almost vertically from the banks of the Madison River. Downstream from the Gneiss Creek trailhead, the Madison Valley is a broad flat plain covered with grass, sage, and aspens. Much of the Madison area was burned to varying degrees in the fires of 1988.

PURPLE MOUNTAIN TRAIL
(3 miles, 5 kilometers)

Calling this a mountain is a bit optimistic, but none-the-less the hike to the top does seem like a long one. The trail climbs 1,500 vertical feet through intermittently burned forest to a pretty good view of the Gibbon River Valley. The best thing about this trail is that it starts close by Madison Campground, about ¼ mile north of Madison Junction on the Madison-Norris Road. *Map 13*

HARLEQUIN LAKE TRAIL
(0.5 mile, 0.8 kilometer)

This short trail starts about 1.5 miles from the Madison Campground on the West Entrance Road. The hike is through a lodgepole pine forest to the small lake which is usually home for a variety of waterfowl, but not harlequin ducks as the name might imply. Large numbers of mosquitoes have also found a home here and can be quite thick until late July. *Map 13*

Dipper
- *on rocks in fast stream*
- *flies low and fast*
- *bobs up and down*

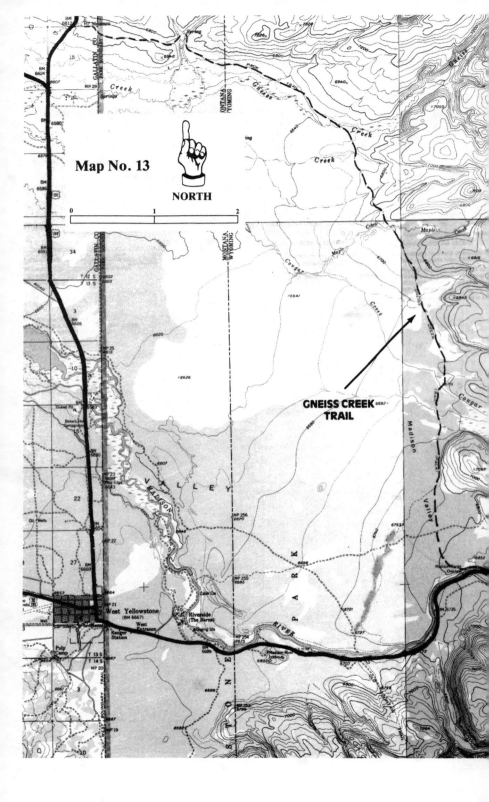

Map No. 13

NORTH

GNEISS CREEK
TRAIL

GNEISS CREEK TRAIL

The Gneiss Creek Trail travels through the flat Madison Valley, among stands of Douglas fir and aspen, and across clear, willow lined creeks. During the summer, chances of seeing moose are excellent. Elk spend the fall, winter, and spring in this area and can sometimes be seen in large numbers. The area is also good grizzly habitat, so take the proper precautions for avoiding bears. Remember that grouse are also abundant in this area and may occasionally explode out of a clump of brush beside the trail and fly away in front of you. To hikers treading cautiously along this trail thinking that a grizzly could be lurking behind any tree, this sudden surprise could cause heart failure or at least require a change of pants.

Madison River Bridge Trailhead to:

Cougar Creek	4 miles	6.5 km
Maple Creek	7	11
Gneiss Creek	9	14.5
Campanula Creek	12	19
Trailhead on Highway 191	14	22

The Gneiss Creek Trail starts from the Madison River Bridge about 7 miles west of Madison Junction on the West Entrance Road. The trail follows the river along the steep cliffs of its north shore for 1 mile then leaves the river and heads north through the forest. The trail continues through intermittently burned sage meadows, aspen and fir forest for the remainder of the hike to Highway 191. The trailhead on this end is located at Fir Ridge Cemetery, milepost 9. This trail has virtually no long hill climbing and the stream crossings are all easily waded after the end of June. Beware. Biting flies can be very unpleasant from mid to late summer.

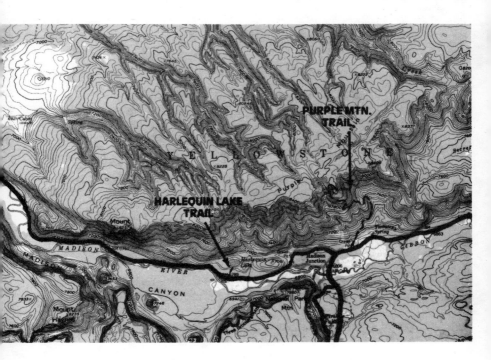

Castle Geyser

FIREHOLE VALLEY AREA

The valley of the Firehole River is probably best known for its thermal areas, which contain the largest concentration of geysers anywhere in the world. There are three main thermal areas along the river. From the north to south they are the Lower, Midway and Upper Geyser Basins. Old Faithful is located in the Upper Geyser Basin. Each of these areas has an abundance of short walkways that offer a close look at a variety of amazing hydrothermal features. A leaflet which describes the Upper Geyser Basin and its many walkways is available from the Old Faithful Visitor Center.

The backcountry trails in the Firehole Valley travel not only to thermal features, but also to waterfalls, lakes, and meadows. Some of the more spectacular of these are Lone Star Geyser, Fairy Falls, and Mystic Falls. In addition to these geologic features, there are also bison and elk which spend the entire year near the Firehole Valley, wintering in the vicinity of the geyser basins and spending their summers feeding in such places as Buffalo Meadows and Little Firehole Meadows.

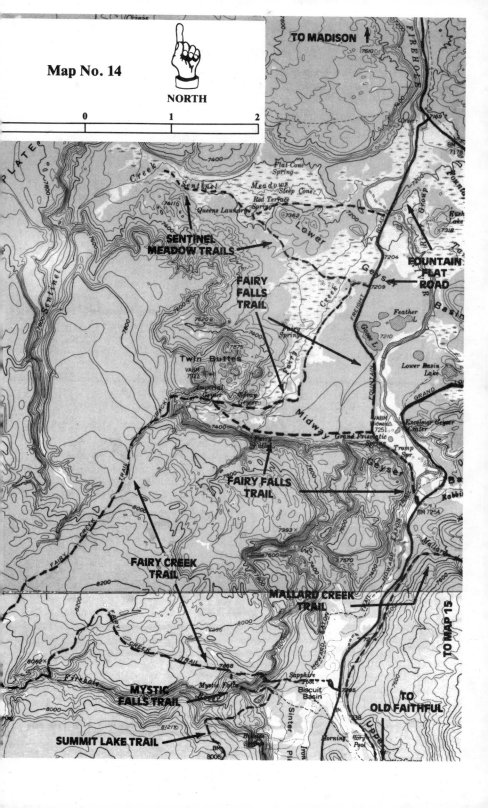

Map No. 14

NORTH

0   1   2

TO MADISON

SENTINEL
MEADOW TRAILS

FAIRY
FALLS
TRAIL

FOUNTAIN
FLAT
ROAD

FAIRY FALLS
TRAIL

FAIRY CREEK
TRAIL

MALLARD CREEK
TRAIL

MYSTIC
FALLS TRAIL

SUMMIT LAKE TRAIL

TO OLD FAITHFUL

TO MAP 15

MYSTIC FALLS TRAIL

From Biscuit Basin Parking Area to:

Little Firehole Meadows Trail Jct.	.6 miles	1 km
Summit Lake Trail Jct.	.6	1
Mystic Falls	1.1	1.8
Top of Mystic Falls	1.4	2.2
Little Firehole Meadows Trail Jct.	1.7	2.7
Scenic Overlook	2.3	3.7
Biscuit Basin Parking Area	3.0	4.8

Mystic Falls is an impressive 100 foot drop of the Little Firehole River as it comes off the Madison Plateau into the Firehole River Valley. The trail to the falls starts at Biscuit Basin (on the Old Faithful-Madison Road). Follow the asphalt and board walkway across the river until the Mystic Falls Trail branches off into the forest. About ⅓ mile further you will come to a trail junction. Here the Summit Lake Trail goes to the left and the Little Firehole Meadows Trail goes to the right. Straight ahead, ½ mile further, is Mystic Falls. From Mystic Falls you climb a series of switchbacks to an excellent view point at the top of the falls. If you want to make this a loop hike (it's only .2 mile further than going back the way you came) continue on this trail until it meets the Little Firehole Meadows Trail. At this junction turn right and descend to an overlook; here it is possible to view a far away eruption of Old Faithful. Continue on Little Firehole Meadows Trail downhill until you rejoin the Mystic Falls Trail which takes you back to Biscuit Basin Parking Area. *Maps 14, 15*

SUMMIT LAKE TRAIL
(7.5 miles, 12 kilometers)

The Summit Lake Trail starts from Biscuit Basin and follows the Mystic Falls Trail for about ½ mile. After branching south from that trail, the Summit Lake Trail crosses Little Firehole River then climbs 600 feet in 1.5 miles to the Madison Plateau. The trail continues to climb gradually as it gains 700 more feet in the remaining 6 miles. Much of this area was burned during the 1988 fires. Summit Lake is almost completely surrounded by trees except for a small meadow. ½ mile west of Summit Lake is the Continental Divide. Here there are some interesting and seldom visited thermal features as well as good views of Idaho's Centennial Range. *Map 15*

TRAILS TO FAIRY FALLS

The 200 foot drop of Fairy Creek makes Fairy Falls one of Yellowstone's highest waterfalls. The small stream of water seems to descend in delicate slow motion. This spectacular falls can be reached by three different short trails.

The longest, but most scenic, route starts at the trailhead 1 mile south of the Firehole River bridge on the Fountain Flat Drive. This 3 mile trail follows Fairy Creek through wet meadows, where elk can be seen all through the year. After the trail crosses Fairy Creek (bridged), it heads west to Imperial Geyser. From this large pool of super heated water, the trail hooks up with the Fairy Creek Trail and follows it east to the base of Fairy Falls.

The trailhead for the second route is reached by driving south on the Fountain Flat Drive until you reach the barricade that prevents further automobile travel. From this point continue by hiking south, past the barricade, along this old road for about 1 mile. Here a trail turns west into the forest and continues to Fairy Falls, 1.5 miles away, making this route a total of 2.5 miles in length.

The third route to Fairy Falls starts from the trailhead 1 mile south of Midway Geyser Basin Parking Area. This route follows a dirt road for about 1 mile and then turns west through the forest to Fairy Falls using the same 1.5 mile trail as the previous hike (which makes this third trail also a total of 2.5 miles in length). *Maps 14, 15*

SENTINEL MEADOWS TRAIL
(1.5 miles, 2.5 km)

Sentinel Meadows has a small thermal area which contains a feature called Queens Laundry Spring. In 1881, under the orders of Yellowstone's second superintendent Phil Norris, work was begun on a bathhouse at this spring. As it so happened, Norris was replaced as superintendent before the bathhouse was finished and work never resumed on this building. This structure's logs have been preserved by the mineral laden water of the hot spring; and thus today this uncompleted bathhouse still remains, although quite dilapidated, as the first government building constructed in any National Park solely for the use of the public.

Sentinel Meadows is an occasional feeding spot for bison from October through early June. Sandhill cranes have been observed nesting in this area in June and may be spotted throughout the summer in the vicinity of the meadows.

There are two trails leading to Sentinel Meadows. The first one of these starts at the Firehole River Bridge on the Fountain Flat drive and travels 1.5 miles to Sentinel Meadows where it joins the second trails. The second trail starts about .5 mile south of the Firehole River Bridge. It crosses the meadows of Fairy Creek, then enters a lodgepole pine forest through which it continues until it emerges into the sedge and grass of Sentinel Meadows. This trail continues about 1 mile further to a campsite along Sentinel Creek (total distance 2.5 miles). *Map 14*

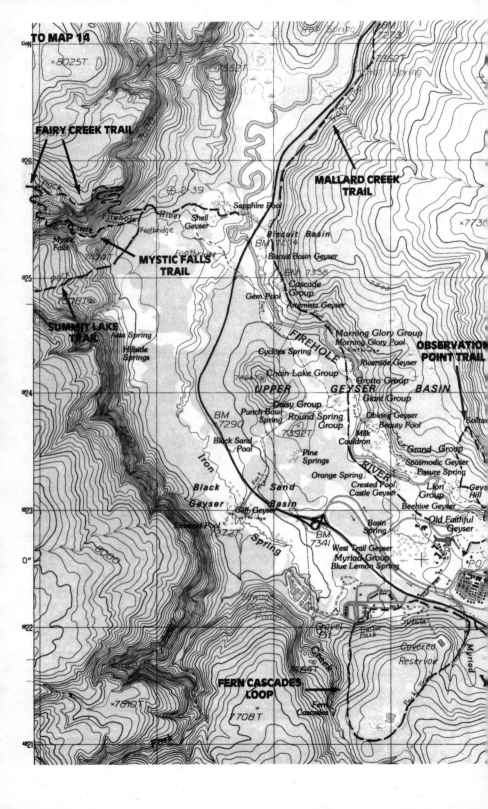

10mN

×8025T

7558T

FAIRY CREEK TRAIL

BM 7273

7862T

MALLARD CREEK TRAIL

Trails Line

326

Hot Spring

Sapphire Pool

Firehole River

Shell Geyser

Footbridge

Footbridge

MYSTIC FALLS TRAIL

Mystic Falls

7834T

Biscuit Basin

BM 7274

Biscuit Basin Geyser

BM 7338

Cascade Group

Gem Pool

Artemisia Geyser

×7730

325

7878T

SUMMIT LAKE TRAIL

Azia Spring

Hillside Springs

Morning Glory Group

Morning Glory Pool

FIREHOLE

Cyclops Spring

Riverside Geyser

OBSERVATION POINT TRAIL

Chain Lake Group

UPPER

GEYSER

Grotto Group

BASIN

324

BM 7290

Punch Bowl Spring

Daisy Group

Giant Group

Round Spring Group

7392T

Oblong Geyser

Beauty Pool

Solitar

Black Sand Pool

Milk Cauldron

Pine Springs

Grand Group

Iron

Orange Spring

Crested Pool

Spasmodic Geyser

Fissure Spring

RIVER

323

Black

Sand

Basin

Castle Geyser

Lion Group

Geyse Hill

Geyser

Cliff Geyser

Footbridge

Basin Spring

Beehive Geyser

Emerald Pool

7721

Spring

BM 7341

West Trail Geyser

Old Faithful Geyser

Myriad Group

Blue Lemon Spring

P.O.

0"

9000

322

Nymph Thermal Pools

Gravel Pit

Tractor Park

Subsla

Covered Reservoir

FERN CASCADES LOOP

Creek

7641

Myriad

×7810T

×7708T

Fern Cascades

Park

321

4921

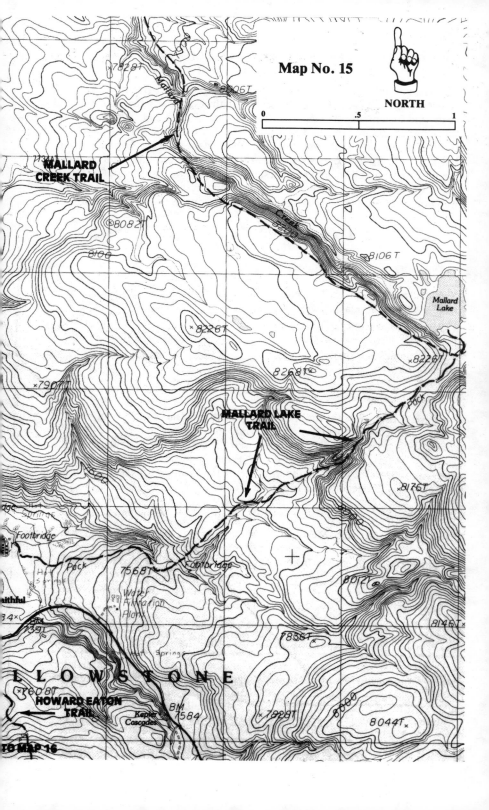

Map No. 15

NORTH

0 .5 1

MALLARD CREEK TRAIL

MALLARD LAKE TRAIL

Mallard Lake

HOWARD EATON TRAIL

Kepler Cascades

BM 7584

TO MAP 16

Footbridge

Footbridge

Spring

FERN CASCADES SEMI-LOOP TRAIL
(1.7 miles, 2.7 km)

This short trail starts in the Old Faithful housing area (from the Old Faithful Ranger Station: follow the service road southwest, across the entrance and exit roads and then across the main road to the housing area) and ends near the start of the Howard Eaton Trail to Lone Star. The Fern Cascades Trail travels entirely through forest and climbs and descends about 200 feet. Fern Cascades are pretty, but not very impressive. A short detour to the west is required to look down into the little canyon and see the cascades. Although it's a great ski trail in the winter, I'd only recommend it in the summer to people staying in the Old Faithful Area who don't have a car, and who have hiked all the other trails in the area. *Map 15*

LITTLE FIREHOLE MEADOWS TRAIL
(Fairy Creek Trail)

The Fairy Creek Trail travels from Biscuit Basin to Little Firehole Meadows, past Imperial Geyser and Fairy Falls, to the trailhead at Midway Geyser Basin. The highlight of the trail is Fairy Falls (which can also be reached by a 2.5 mile hike from the Fountain Flats Drive). *Maps 14, 15*

From Trailhead at Biscuit Basin to:

Mystic Falls Trail Jct.	0.6 miles	1 km
Little Firehole Meadows	5	8
Imperial Geyser	10.2	17
Fairy Falls	11	17.6
Trailhead south of Midway Geyser Basin	13.5	21.6

Starting from Biscuit Basin (2 miles north of Old Faithful on the road to Madison Junction), the Fairy Creek Trail follows the Mystic Falls Trail for ½ mile until it branches off uphill to the west. The Fairy Creek Trail climbs steeply, 400 vertical feet, up open rocky slopes. From these slopes, it's possible to watch Old Faithful geyser erupt in the distance to the southeast. The trail continues to climb through lodgepole pine forest for 2 more miles. It then descends to the Little Firehole River just downstream from a lovely waterfall. From this point the trail follows the river upstream, about ½ mile to Little Firehole Meadows.

The Little Firehole Meadows is a summering spot for bison. You may occasionally see the bison from the trail, but often they're feeding on parts of the meadow that aren't visible from the beaten path. Even if you don't see the bison themselves, you're certain to see such evidence of their presence as droppings (careful where you step) and trees that have had the bark stripped and whole branches removed by the bison's horning.

The Fairy Creek Trail follows the eastern edge of the meadows about ¼ mile and then re-enters the forest. From Little Firehole Meadows, the trail descends gradually until it reaches the edge of the Madison Plateau where it drops about 400 feet in ½ mile. Once at the bottom of the plateau, the trail passes Imperial Geyser which is a large pool of boiling water that is almost constantly erupting. A short ways past Imperial Geyser, the trail branches. One trail heads north along Fairy Creek to the Fountain Flat Drive. The other trail travels to Fairy Falls and the Midway Geyser Basin Trailhead (see "Trails to Fairy Falls" section).

Canada Goose

LONE STAR GEYSER TRAIL

Lone Star Trailhead to:

Lone Star Geyser	2.3 miles	3.7 km
Jct. with Bechler River Trail	6.5	10.5
Shoshone Lake	8.5	13.5

The Lone Star Trailhead is located just south of Kepler Cascades, 3.5 miles from Old Faithful overpass on the Old Faithful-West Thumb Road. This route is also a partly-paved bike trail as far as Lone Star Geyser. No bicycle travel is allowed beyond Lone Star Geyser, or off of the Lone Star Geyser Trail. The level trail follows the Firehole River the entire way and is an easy, pleasant hike. Lone Star Geyser erupts about every 3 hours from its 12 foot high cone. The eruptions are usually 30-50 feet high and are followed by a roaring steam phase.

The Shoshone Lake Trail continues from Lone Star up to Grants Pass and down to the Bechler River Trail and Shoshone Lake. *Maps 15, 16*

HOWARD EATON TRAIL TO LONE STAR GEYSER
(3.1 miles, 5 kilometers)

This trail starts about ¾ mile from Old Faithful overpass on the Old Faithful-West Thumb Road, just east of a service road. (The service road starts at the Old Faithful Ranger Station, behind the Visitor Center parking lot). Look for the orange markers. This route leads up, over and down a 500 foot forested hill to Lone Star Geyser. This trail is longer, much steeper, not as scenic, and thus, less travelled than the other Lone Star Trail. The one advantage to this trail is that it provides access to Lone Star Geyser from the Old Faithful Area without having to drive to a trailhead. Much of this area was burned during the 1988 fires. *Maps 15, 16*

OBSERVATION POINT LOOP TRAIL
(2 miles, 3 kilometers)

Although not really a backcountry trail, this is one of the best short trails in the park. It provides a great overlook to view an eruption of Old Faithful, a walk past interesting thermal features and a good look at the Firehole River. Before starting on the trail, check at O.F. Visitor Center for the next scheduled eruption of Old Faithful, and time your hike accordingly. The trail starts at the Old Faithful Visitor Center and follows the Geyser Hill Trail around Old Faithful Geyser and across the Firehole River. On the north side of the river, the Observation Point Trail starts climbing steadily along switchbacks (160 vertical feet) to Observation Point. From the overlook, the trail descends about 0.3 mile down to Solitary Geyser, then continues on down to the Geyser Hill Trail, and back to the Visitor Center. *Map 15*

MALLARD LAKE TRAIL

From Trailhead at Old Faithful Lodge to:

Jct. with Ridge Trail	3.1 miles	5 km
Mallard Lake	3.3	5.3
Grand Loop Road and Jct. with trail back to Old Faithful	7.5	12
Morning Glory Pool	10.3	17
Old Faithful Visitor Center	11.7	18.7

The trailhead for the Mallard Lake Trail is located between the Old Faithful Lodge's cabins and the Firehole River. There is a small bridge across the river at this spot. From the bridge, the trail climbs gradually through a lodgepole pine forest passing Pipeline Hotsprings which contains some small mud pots. After 2.5 miles the trail winds through an open rocky area. Here the cliffs on either side of the trail are composed of rhyolite, as is the entire Central Plateau upon which the Mallard Lake Trail rests. From the junction with the Ridge Trail (Mallard Creek Trail) it is a little over a tenth of a mile to Mallard Lake. The lake is surrounded by lodgepole pine. Waterfowl can usually be seen swimming and diving in its cold waters.

If you continue on the Ridge Trail you'll climb steeply to a good overlook of Mallard Lake and the Mallard Creek Canyon. Much of this area was burned during the 1988 fires. Approximately 2 miles further down the trail you'll descend into the canyon of Mallard Creek. Here the creek is a lovely little warm water cascade. The trail then ascends to the top of the north side of the canyon. From this point there is a view to the west of the Twin Buttes. Near the 7.4 mile point you'll come to a junction. The trail to the right leads to Fairy Falls about 3 miles away. The trail to the left leads to Old Faithful. The trail to Old Faithful will parallel the road south (following the power lines part of the way) until it hits the old road back to Morning Glory Pool. From Morning Glory you follow the asphalt trail, passing Riverside and Castle Geyser, back to the Old Faithful Visitor Center. *Map 15*

SHOSHONE LAKE AREA

Shoshone Lake, Yellowstone's largest backcountry lake, has attracted backcountry travelers and explorers for hundreds of years. During this time, it's had many names. It was called Snake Lake by the mountain men of the fur trading era who referred to the Shoshone Indians as the "Snake" Indians; called Madison Lake by those that erroneously thought it drained into the Madison River; called DeLacy Lake in honor of the first man to map the lake as flowing into the Snake River; and finally called Shoshone Lake to acknowledge the earliest name used by the fur trappers.

Shoshone Lake and its shoreline are home for a variety of finned, furred and feathered creatures. Its cold deep waters hold brown, brook and lake trout. These non native species were introduced into this formerly fishless lake during the 1890's. Waterbirds gather on, and around, the lake to feed on these fish and other aquatic animals and plants. Ospreys, California gulls, Barrow's goldeneye, mallards, scaups, common mergansers, coots, spotted sandpipers, and American avocets can be spotted in this area. Sandhill cranes may or may not be seen, but they're often heard for miles as they call out in a voice that's described as a low, loud, musical rattle. Moose are common to the area and elk and deer are occasionally seen in shoreline meadows. If you're lucky, you may spot a weasel chasing shorebirds across a beach or otters frolicking and fishing in the lake. Mosquitoes can be amazingly numerous from late June to late July. Insect netting on tents, and mosquito repellent are necessities here.

On Shoshone Lake's west shore is Shoshone Geyser Basin, which has a number of interesting active geysers. The most impressive is Union Geyser which erupts from three vents simultaneously. Intervals between eruptions are irregular so it will take some waiting and quite a bit of luck to catch an eruption of Union. Remember that the geyser basin has areas with thin crusts and superheated water. In 1988 a young man was burned to death from falling into one of these hot pools. Fear and caution should be your guide if walking off trail in the thermal area. These places can be very dangerous.

Osborne Russell described walking through Shoshone Geyser Basin in his journal kept during the 1830's. He wrote, "On a near approach we could hear the water bubbling underground some distance from the surface. The sound of our footsteps over this place was like thumping over a hollow vessel of immense size..." It's quite a feeling to walk through a spot and experience the same thing that someone else experienced 150 years earlier.

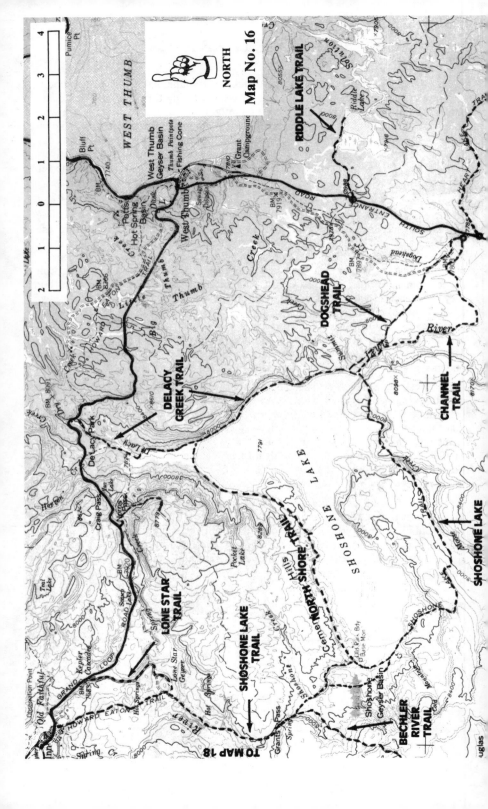

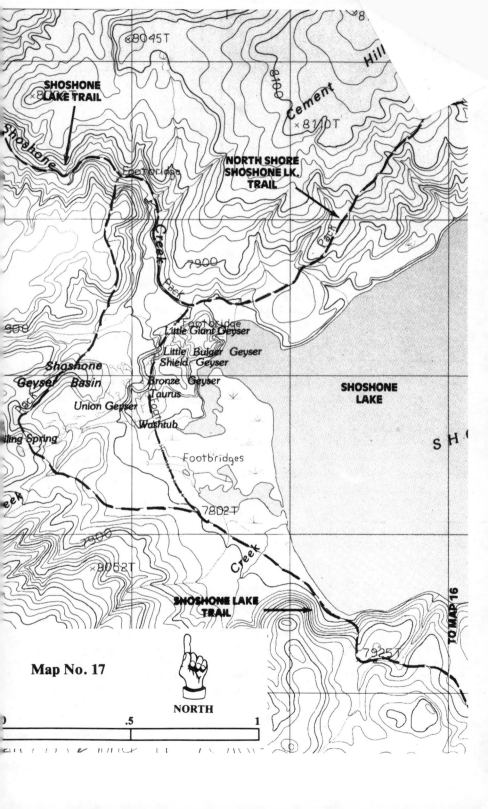

SHOSHONE
LAKE TRAIL

×8045T

Cement
Hill

×8110T

Shoshone

Footbridge

NORTH SHORE
SHOSHONE LK.
TRAIL

Creek

Pack

7900

Pack

Footbridge
Little Giant Geyser

SHOSHONE
LAKE

Shoshone
Geyser Basin

Little Bulger Geyser
Shield Geyser
Bronze Geyser
Taurus

Pack

Union Geyser

Washtub

S H O

iling Spring

Footbridges

eek

7802T

×8052T

7900

Creek

SHOSHONE LAKE
TRAIL

7925T

TO MAP 16

Map No. 17

NORTH

0   .5   1

SHOSHONE LAKE TRAIL

Lone Star Trailhead (just south of Kepler Cascades on the Old Faithful-West Thumb Road) to:

Lone Star Geyser	3 miles	5 km
Grants Pass	6	9.5
Jct. with Bechler Trail	6.5	10.5
Jct. with Horse By-pass	7.7	12.3
Jct. with North Shore Trail	8.3	13.3
Shoshone Geyser Basin	8.5	13.6
Moose Creek	15	24
Lewis Channel	17.5	28
Dogshead Trailhead	22	35

Starting from the Lone Star Trailhead, the Shoshone Lake Trail follows the bike path along the Firehole River to Lone Star Geyser. From the geyser, the trail crosses the Firehole River by bridge and then follows the river past hot springs, through a forest and out into a meadow, where elk and bison are occasionally seen during spring and fall. The trail then re-enters the forest and climbs moderately (300 feet) to Grants Pass. From the pass the trail descends to the junction with the Bechler River Trail. The Shoshone Trail continues down towards the lake, crossing Shoshone Creek by bridge, and meeting the Horse By-pass Trail (This 2 miles trail skirts around the Shoshone Geyser Basin and joins back up with the Shoshone Lake Trail further south).

From the Horse Trail junction, the Shoshone Lake Trail continues along Shoshone Creek and then to the junction with the North Shore Trail (the North Shore Trail veers east). The Shoshone Lake Trail soon enters the Shoshone Geyser Basin, one of Yellowstone's most spectacular backcountry thermal areas. The trail takes you by a number of geysers, hot springs and interesting meadows, and then meets up with the south junction of the Horse By-pass Trail.

Leaving the lake, the trail climbs over a lodgepole pine covered ridge to the meadows of Moose Creek. Although thick with mosquitoes during July, these meadows may offer a good opportunity to see elk and moose feeding during the evenings. The Shoshone Lake Trail continues along Moose Creek and crosses it in a narrow valley. This crossing is about calf deep after midsummer and there is often a log on which to cross. From the crossing of Moose Creek, the trail climbs over two low ridges to the outlet of Shoshone Lake. You'll begin to see the effects of the fires of 1988 in this area. The crossing of Lewis Channel is about knee deep during the summer.

After the channel crossing, The Shoshone Lake Trail follows the eastern shore of Shoshone Lake through a meadow for about ¼ mile. You will come to the junction with the Lewis Channel Trail. (The Channel Trail heads east 7 miles to the Dogshead Trailhead). The Shoshone Lake Trail continues north. ¼ mile further you will reach the junction with the Dogshead Trail and the Delacy Creek Trail. The Dogshead Trail goes southeast 4 miles to the Dogshead Trailhead on the South Entrance Road. The Delacy Creek Trail follows the east shore of Shoshone Lake to Delacy Creek and on to the trailhead on the Old Faithful-West Thumb Road.

Maps 16, 17

DELACY CREEK TRAIL

DeLacy Trailhead to:

Shoshone Lake	3 miles	5 km
Lewis Channel	7.5	12
Lewis Trailhead	12	19

The DeLacy Creek Trail travels from Delacy Trailhead (about 8 miles east of Old Faithful on the Old Faithful-West Thumb Road) to the junction with the Shoshone Lake Trail at the Lewis River Channel. The first 3 miles of this trail is especially nice, and provides a short route to Shoshone Lake.

The trail starts out through forest with Delacy Creek winding along side. After about a mile the trail leaves the forest and enters the open meadows of the creek. Both coyotes and moose are commonly seen in these meadows, along with sandhill cranes, mallards and other waterfowl that frequent the waters of DeLacy Creek. The trail continues to follow the edge of the forest and meadows all the way to the shoreline of Shoshone Lake. Once at Shoshone Lake the trail travels south along the forested shoreline. About 2 miles from Lewis Channel the trail climbs about 100 feet to a good view, through the burned trees, of Shoshone Lake. The trail then descends to the junction with the Shoshone Lake Trail and the Dogshead Trail. The Dogshead Trail leads to the South Entrance Road 4 miles away. *Map 16*

Barrow's Goldeneye

SHOSHONE LAKE NORTH SHORE TRAIL
(7 miles, 11 kilometers)

This trail travels from the Shoshone Geyser Basin area to the DeLacy Creek Trail. The entire trail is in lodgepole pine forest and is relatively level; although one 200 foot ridge is climbed about midway on the trail. The trail offers good views of the lake from cliffs above the shoreline. *Map 16*

DOGSHEAD TRAIL TO SHOSHONE LAKE
(4 miles, 6.5 kilometers)

The Dogshead Trail is the shortest route into Shoshone Lake from the South Entrance Road. It leaves from Dogshead Trailhead (just north of Lewis Lake on the west side of the South Entrance Road) and travels through forest burned by the fires of 1988. It climbs gradually about 200 vertical feet up and over a forested ridge and then down to the junction with the Shoshone Lake Trail and the DeLacy Creek Trail. *Map 16*

LEWIS CHANNEL TRAIL
(7 miles, 11 kilometers)

This trail travels from Dogshead Trailhead (just north of Lewis Lake on the west side of the South Entrance Road) to Shoshone Lake. It follows Lewis Channel and provides a longer, but more scenic, route than the Dogshead Trail. The trail travels through sections of forest burned by the 1988 fires. From the trailhead the Lewis Channel Trail follows the Dogshead Trail then turns to the left and heads south towards Lewis Lake. Look for huckleberry bushes in this area, usually ripening in late August through September. From the lake shore the trail heads west towards the Lewis Channel and follows it for about the last 3.5 miles to Shoshone Lake. This scenic section of trail is used mainly by fishermen, but is quite worthwhile even if you don't have a rod and reel. The trail ends at the junction with the Shoshone Lake Trail. By following this trail north you can join the Dogshead Trail and loop back to Dogshead Trailhead. *Map 16*

DIVIDE LOOKOUT TRAIL
(2.5 miles, 4 kilometers)

The Divide Lookout Trail starts at the trailhead and parking area 6.7 miles east of the Old Faithful intersection on the Old Faithful-West Thumb Road. The trail climbs 700 vertical feet through forest to a 70 foot high lookout tower. You can climb the stairs of the tower, but a locked trap door prevents you from going up to the observation deck. Still, the view from the steps is marvelous. Shoshone Lake and Mt. Sheridan to the southeast, the Teton Range to the south, and Yellowstone Lake to the east are all visible. The tower is 8,779 feet above sea level. *Map 16*

RIDDLE LAKE TRAIL
(2.5 miles, 4 km)

The Riddle Lake Trail starts at the trailhead approximately 3 miles south of Grant Village intersection. Even though it crosses the Continental Divide, the trail is very level. The Riddle Lake Trail travels mainly through small meadows where moose are often spotted. Intermittent streams through these meadows make the going very mushy until the middle of July. Riddle Lake is a lovely little lake with a shoreline changing from marsh to rock to sandy beach. The Red Mountains and Mt. Sheridan provide a scenic backdrop as you hike along the lake's north shore. Sandpipers, Barrow's goldeneye, sandhill cranes, Canada geese and even white pelicans are seen around Riddle Lake. The marshes are a haven for mosquitoes, which can be quite a nuisance throughout July. *Maps 19, 20*

BECHLER RIVER AND FALLS RIVER AREA

This area of Yellowstone is also called the Cascade Corner, a fitting name for an area that contains over half of all the park's waterfalls. Fed by creeks and rivers coming off the Madison and Pitchstone Plateaus, many of these falls drop over 100 feet. The highest is Union Falls at 250 feet. Although not as high as Union, Cave Falls, Colonnade Falls, Ouzel Falls, Dunanda Falls, and the many others in this area are all magnificent sights.

The Bechler River and Falls River Area is lower and wetter than most of Yellowstone. Consequently the vegetation consists of more than just lodgepole pine. For instance, you may find: Douglas fir, aspen and willows in Bechler Meadows; Engleman spruce, huckleberry, raspberry, thimble berry, ferns and mosses in Bechler Canyon; and buffalo berry, gooseberry, and mountain ash along the Falls River and Mountain Ash Creek.

Wildlife viewing opportunities in the area are varied. Black bear, moose, mule deer, elk, sandhill cranes, and great blue herons are some of the more impressive animals seen in the Bechler River and Falls River Area. Bears frequent the berry patches found in Bechler Canyon. The cranes, herons, and moose are often seen in the Bechler Meadows, while the deer and elk may be seen just about anywhere.

Because the area is so wet, the most enjoyable time to hike here is during the fall when the meadows have dried up, the streams gone down, and the mosquitoes thinned out. Mosquitoes and biting flies can be overwhelming in this area from mid June to early August.

Many of the trails in this area start from either the Bechler Ranger Station or Cave Falls. To reach Cave Falls you must drive east 26 miles from Ashton, Idaho on the Cave Falls Road. The Bechler Ranger Station is reached by turning off the Cave Falls Road about 3 miles before the road ends at Cave Falls. From this turnoff, follow the gravel road 1.5 miles to the ranger station.

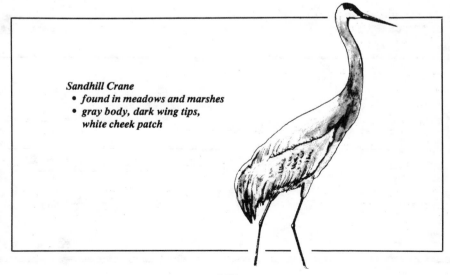

Sandhill Crane
- *found in meadows and marshes*
- *gray body, dark wing tips, white cheek patch*

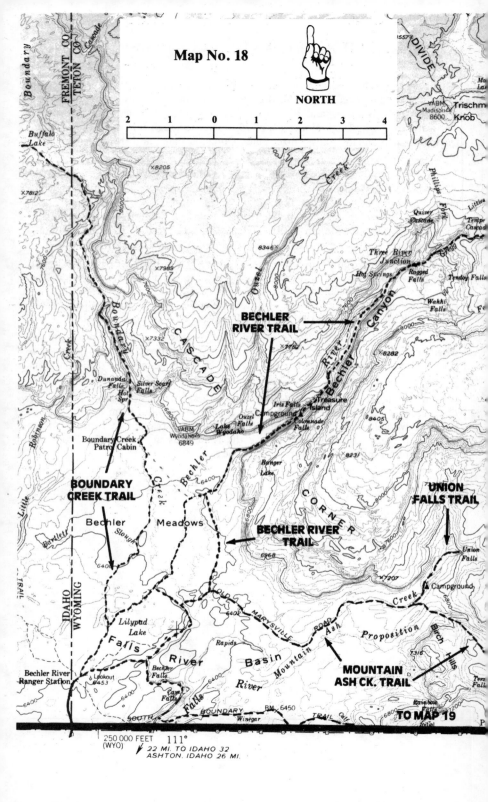

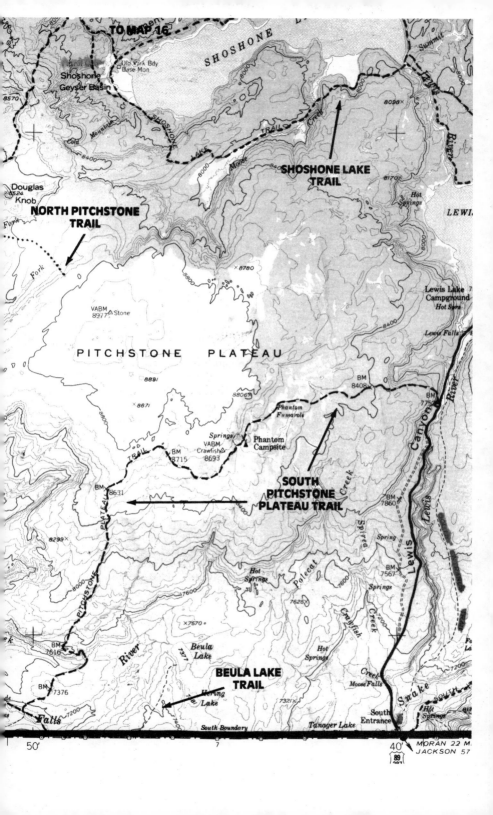

TO MAP 16

SHOSHONE

Shoshone Geyser Basin

Old Park Bdy Base Mon

8570

Cold Mountain

8400

Moose Creek

TRAILS

Douglas Knob 8524

NORTH PITCHSTONE TRAIL

Fork

Fork

SHOSHONE LAKE TRAIL

8098×

8170

Hot Springs

LEWIS

× 8780

8800

× 8977 Stone

VABM

PITCHSTONE PLATEAU

8891

8871

8806

Lewis Lake Campground
Hot Spgs

Lewis Falls

88062

BM 8408

8400

BM 7752

Phantom Fumarole

Springs
VABM Crawfish 8693

TRAIL

Phantom Campsite

8715

SOUTH PITCHSTONE PLATEAU TRAIL

Creek

BM 8631

PLATEAU

8299×

PITCHSTONE

8000

Hot Springs

7600

Spirea Creek

BM 7860

Spring

Spring

BM 7567

Springs

Polecat

×7570

×7626

7600

Hot Springs

BM 7616

River

Beula Lake

7377

BEULA LAKE TRAIL

Hot Springs

Crawfish Creek

Lewis

Canyon

River

BM 7376

Falls

7200

Herring Lake

7321×

South Boundary

7600

Moose Falls

Creek

Snake

Tanager Lake

South Entrance

Hot Springs

50'

7

40'

MORAN 22 M.
JACKSON 57

89

BECHLER RIVER TRAIL

The Bechler (pronounced "bek-ler") River Trail provides access to the most spectacular display of waterfalls and cascades found anywhere in Yellowstone. Cave Falls, Bechler Falls, Colonnade and Iris Falls, Ragged Falls, Twister Falls, and others are all located along this exciting trail. The trail also travels through Bechler Meadows, which is excellent wildlife habitat, especially for moose, mule deer, cranes, and herons. Bechler Meadows can be quite mucky, and mosquitoes can be quite numerous, through the end of July. From Bechler Meadows the trail travels through the lush forest of Bechler Canyon up to the Madison Plateau, then up and over Grants Pass and down to the Firehole River past Lone Star Geyser. *Map 18*

Cave Falls to:		
Bechler Falls	1 miles	1.5 km
Jct. with Mtn. Ash Creek Tr.	3.5	5.3
Boundary Creek (foot bridge)	5	8
Bechler Ford (foot bridge)	7	11
Colonnade Falls	10.5	17
Three Rivers Junction	14.8	23.7
Douglas Knob	18.9	30.2
Jct. with Shoshone Lake Trail	24.5	39.2
Lone Star Geyser	27.5	44
Lone Star Trailhead	30	48

From the south there are two starting points for the Bechler River Trail. The most scenic route starts from Cave Falls (at the end of the Cave Falls Road, 26 miles east from Ashton, Idaho). This route follows the Bechler River past Bechler Falls. The other route starts at the Bechler Ranger Station. From the station you follow the Bechler Meadows Trail until it joins the actual Bechler River Trail in Bechler Meadows.

The actual Bechler River Trail starts at Cave Falls and travels upstream to Rocky Ford where it makes an unbridged crossing of the Bechler River. The Bechler River Trail then travels along the east side of the river until it joins the Bechler Meadows Trail near the Bechler Ford foot bridge. I feel there is a better route which is more scenic and avoids the unbridged crossing of Bechler River at Rocky Ford: This route follows the Bechler River Trail to Rocky Ford where instead of crossing the river, it turns left off the Bechler River Trail and follows the Rocky Ford cutoff trail to Bechler Meadows Trail. The route then follows the Bechler Meadows Trail, crosses Boundary Creek (foot bridge), and leads to the Bechler Ford footbridge. Here the Bechler Meadows Trail rejoins the actual Bechler River Trail, and the Bechler River Trail is taken up through Bechler Canyon. This is the route for which mileages are given in the table above. (The Bechler Ford can also be reached directly from the Bechler Ranger Station via the Bechler Meadows Trail. This route cuts about 2 miles off the above mileages but does not offer the views of Cave Falls, Bechler Falls, and the Bechler River.)

From the Bechler Ford bridge the trail leaves the river and winds through Douglas fir forest and meadows for about 1 mile until it again reaches the river and enters the Bechler Canyon. From this point the trail follows the river past Colonnade and Iris Falls and up to Three Rivers Junction. Along this section of

126

the route there has been recent trail construction that has allowed hikers to stay on the east side of the Bechler River and avoid the 2 crossings that formerly had to be made. Horse parties must still use the old section of trail and make the two crossings.

Three Rivers Junction is the confluence of Phillips Fork, Gregg Fork, and Ferris Fork and is a popular camping area. The Bechler River Trail crosses the Ferris Fork just below Ragged Falls. Because of runoff from hot springs upstream, the water in this creek is warm. After crossing Ferris Fork, the Bechler River Trail climbs 600 feet in 2 miles along the Gregg Fork, crossing it once about ¼ mile above Twister Falls. From Twister Falls the trail climbs about 300 more feet up to the base of Douglas Knob. After passing Douglas Knob, the trail goes through the meadows of the Littles Fork where moose are often spotted. From these meadows the trail climbs gradually through forest up to the Continental Divide. The trail then descends into a small valley and climbs out the other side over another section of the Continental Divide. From this ridge, The Bechler River Tail heads downhill, losing about 700 feet of elevation in the 2 miles to the junction with the Shoshone Lake Trail. From this junction (you're now actually following the Shoshone Lake Trail back to the trailhead), the trail makes a short easy climb up to Grants Pass, which will be your third crossing of the Continental Divide. It's all downhill from here as the trail descends through forest to the Firehole River and follows it out past Lone Star Geyser to the Lone Star Trailhead.

BOUNDARY CREEK TRAIL

From Bechler Ranger Station to:

Boundary Creek	5 miles	8 km
Dunanda Falls	9	14.4
Buffalo Lake	16	25.6

Starting from Bechler Ranger Station this trail actually follows the Bechler Meadows Trail for the first 1.9 miles. After branching off the Bechler Meadows Trail, the Boundary Creek Trail continues through forest and past intermittent meadows and ponds until it emerges in Bechler Meadows. Here it makes a bridged crossing of Bartlett Slough. Moose are often spotted in this area. A mile from Bartlett Slough the trail crosses Boundary Creek on a footbridge.

Once across Boundary Creek, the trail follows the creek upstream through meadows where sandhill cranes and great blue herons are occasionally seen. After following Boundary Creek about a mile, the trail leaves the creek and travels upstream along one if its tributaries. The Boundary Creek Trail Follows this meandering stream about 1 mile, makes a bridged crossing, and heads through the forest to Silver Scarf Falls. From Silver Scarf Falls a spur trail leads about 200 feet west to the brink of Dunanda Falls. Both of these falls are quite impressive, but Silver Scarf Falls does lose much of its water by the end of the summer.

From Silver Scarf Falls, the trail travels up through the forested canyon on Boundary Creek and gains about 400 feet in the first 2 miles past the falls. The trail continues to climb, but more gradually, as it follows Boundary Creek (crossing it 3 times) to a large meadow. Here the trail leaves the creek and travels northwest through the forest to Buffalo Lake. Buffalo Lake is a small meadow-like lake which is home to a wide variety of waterfowl including avocets, grebes, scaups, mallards, and cranes. Moose are also commonly seen in this area. *Map 18*

Union Falls

TRAILS TO UNION FALLS

Formed as two creeks merge and plunge simultaneously 250 feet over the edge of the Pitchstone Plateau, Union Falls is one of Yellowstone's most impressive waterfalls. There are two routes to Union Falls. Both routes use the Mountain Ash Creek Trail which travels from the end of the Cave Falls Road to Grassy Lake Reservoir on the Ashton Flagg Ranch Road. Obviously you can start at either end of this trail to reach Union Falls, which is linked to the Mountain Ash Creek trail by a 2 mile spur trail called the Union Falls Trail.

GRASSY LAKE TO UNION FALLS
(Via Mountain Ash Creek Trail)

From Grassy Lake Reservoir to:

Proposition Creek	5 miles	8 km
Mountain Ash Creek	5.5	9
Union Falls	7.5	12

This is the shortest route to Union Falls. Grassy Lake Reservoir is reached by taking the Ashton-Flagg Ranch Road from the turnoff on highway 89 (the first left turn north of Flagg Ranch), about 2.5 miles south of Yellowstone's South Entrance. The Mountain Ash Creek Trail starts just north of the dam, by the reservoirs's outlet stream. It follows this stream for ⅛ of a mile, then crosses it. Log jams can usually be found to cross in this area. The trail continues through the woods another mile to the ford of the Falls River. This wide ford can be thigh deep and swift before mid July. After that, it subsides to an easy, but slippery, knee deep crossing (wading shoes are a big help here).

After the ford, the trail climbs gradually up to the junction with the Pitchstone Plateau Trail. The trail continues to climb 200 feet to the top of this lodgepole pine and whortleberry covered ridge. After staying along the top of this broad ridge for 2 miles, the trail descends steeply 600 ft to Proposition Creek where you may see monkshood, paintbrush, sticky geranium and other flowers blooming (July to early August). Fallen logs allow an easy crossing of the creek.

From Proposition Creek, the trail climbs up and over another 200 foot ridge to the trail junction at Mountain Ash Creek. The Mountain Ash Creek continues west to Cave Falls, and the Union Falls Trail turns northeast (right). The Union Falls Trail follows Mountain Ash Creek upstream and then crosses it by bridge after ½ mile. Here a small unnamed creek joins Mountain Ash Creek from the west. Feel this stream's water and notice its warmth. This is due to some impressive hot springs upstream. The Union Falls Trail ends near the top of the falls. Getting to the base of the falls can be tricky, as there is no trail and the steep slope is slippery due to the spray from the falls. *Map 19*

CAVE FALLS TO UNION FALLS
(Via Mountain Ash Creek Trail)

Of the two routes to Union Falls this is the more scenic. It's also longer, but doesn't require as much climbing. Part of this trail follows the old Marysville Road, a wagon road built by the Mormons in the 1880's, which ran from Marysville, Idaho to Jackson Hole, Wyoming. *Maps 18, 19*

Cave Falls to:

Rocky Ford	3.2 miles	5 km
Mountain Ash Creek	8	13
Jct. with Union Falls Trail	9.5	15
Union Falls	11.5	18

Cave Falls is reached by taking U.S. Highway 20 to Ashton, Idaho, then driving east 26 miles on the Cave Falls Road. The trail starts at Cave Falls, which is an impressive drop of the deep and wide Falls River, and follows the Falls River upstream for ¼ mile to the confluence with the Bechler River. The trail then follows the spruce-lined Bechler River upstream past Bechler Falls and a spur trail that heads west to the Bechler Ranger Station. At Rocky Ford, the trail crosses the Bechler River on a slippery rock bottom. The crossing is about knee deep after midsummer and tennis shoes are a real advantage for wading here.

From the ford, the trail travels through forests of Engleman spruce, Douglas Fir, and lodgepole pine and through meadows of grasses, sedges and willows. Mule deer and moose can often be seen feeding in these meadows throughout the summer. Elk may be seen during the fall. Upon reaching Mountain Ash Creek, a knee deep crossing is made and the trail continues to the junction with the Union Falls Trail. Follow the Union Falls Trail upstream along Mountain Ash Creek, crossing it once, until the trail ends near the top of Union Falls.

PITCHSTONE PLATEAU TRAILS

The Pitchstone Plateau is an immense solidified lava flow. The top of the plateau, which varies from 8,600 feet to 8,900 feet above sea level, is for the most part treeless. Instead, grasses and volcanic rock outcrops predominate. The plateau is bordered by thick forest; and growing along the edge of this forest are thousands of young lodgepole pines. These lodgepole are slowly encroaching upon the meadows of the plateau and may eventually cover much of them. But in the meantime, bison spend part of the summer feeding on the grasses up here and you may see signs of their visit (droppings and mutilated trees that have been used for head scratching). Elk and mule deer are also occasionally seen feeding on the plateau during the summer.

There are two trails that travel on the Pitchstone Plateau. The South Pitchstone Plateau Trail traverses the southeast corner of the plateau and the North Pitchstone Plateau Trail is a spur trail from the Bechler River Trail up to the northwest corner of the plateau. Cross country travel is possible due to the open terrain, but should be discussed with rangers at either South Entrance Ranger Station or Bechler Ranger Station. Camping is allowed only at designated campsites and requires a permit. Hikers should also be wary for compass variances due to metallic interference on the plateau. As a final note, this area usually receives heavy snows during the winter and consequently may not be easily accessible before the snow melts in mid July.

SOUTH PITCHSTONE PLATEAU TRAIL

From Trailhead on South Entrance Road to:

Phantom Fumarole	4.5 miles	6 km
Phantom Campsite	5.5	9
Benchmark 8715	8	13
Proposition Creek	14.5	23
Mountain Ash Creek Trail	16.5	26
Grassy Lake Reservoir	18	29

From the South Entrance Road, the trail starts at the trailhead about 2 miles south of Lewis Falls. The trail climbs steeply at first and then more gradually as it nears the open grassland of the plateau. It reaches Phantom Fumarole after about 4.5 miles. This is a small thermal area containing steam vents and mudpots. A mile further, the trail reaches a cold water spring, shown on old maps as Phantom Campsite. Elk, mule deer, and coyotes all frequent this area for water, If you don't see them you'll surely see their tracks.

From the spring, the trail continues to climb, as it again enters the open grassland. The highest point of the trail (8,715') is reached after about 2.5 miles from the spring. There are good views of the Falls River Basin to the southwest, The Grand Tetons to the south and Mt. Sheridan to the northeast.(Much of the trail above treeline, which is marked with rock cairns, may be hard to follow due to the little use it receives). The Pitchstone Plateau Trail then descends gradually about 1,200 feet in 6.5 miles to Proposition Creek. After a log crossing of the creek, the trail continues to descend through forest to the Mountain Ash Creek Trail. From this junction it is 1.5 miles out to the Ashton-Flagg Road. *Maps 18, 19*

NORTH PITCHSTONE PLATEAU TRAIL
(2 miles, 3.2 km)

The North Pitchstone Plateau Trail starts from the Bechler River Trail in a meadow about ½ mile above Twister Falls on the Gregg Fork. This junction is about 16 miles from Bechler Ranger Station. The trail climbs, about 600 vertical feet in 2 miles, through the forest to the tree line and top of the plateau. The maintained trail ends at this point. It is possible, although not encouraged by the National Park Service, to travel cross country to the South Pitchstone Trail and make a loop hike back to Bechler Ranger Station. (It is easier to find the South Trail from the North Trail than vice versa). Check with either Bechler Ranger Station or South Entrance Ranger Station for details and permission for this trip. *Map 18*

SOUTH BOUNDARY TRAIL

The South Boundary Trail travels from the Bechler Ranger Station to the South Entrance Ranger Station; but because the trail was designed for boundary patrol rather than scenic hiking, only the two most interesting portions of that trail have been included in this guide book.

CALF CREEK TO CAVE FALLS

Calf Creek Meadows on Reclamation Road to:

Falls River	2.7 miles	4 km
Winegar Lake	4	6
Cave Falls Road	6.7	11

The Calf Creek meadow is reached by taking the Reclamation Road (Ashton to Flagg Ranch Road) from the turnoff on U.S. Highway 89 between Flagg Ranch and Yellowstone's South Entrance (first left turn north of Flagg Ranch). Follow this paved-then gravel road to Calf Creek Meadows (about 4 miles west of Grassy Lake Reservoir). The trail starts on the north side of Calf Creek, following it downstream through a steep forested draw. It crosses the creek several times on fallen logs. The trail emerges from the forest into the meadows of the Falls River. Moose and elk often make an appearance in the late spring and fall. The trail follows the Falls River (which is inhabited by cutthroat trout) for a short ways then veers off to the meadows of Junco Lake and over past Winegar Lake. Winegar Lake is actually about ¼ mile south of the trail in a grass and sedge meadow.

The trail travels the remaining 3 miles through forest while descending about 300 feet to the Falls River. To reach the Cave Falls Road, a broad, knee deep ford of the Falls River must be negotiated. This ford will be much higher, and probably impassable, before mid July. *Maps 18, 19*

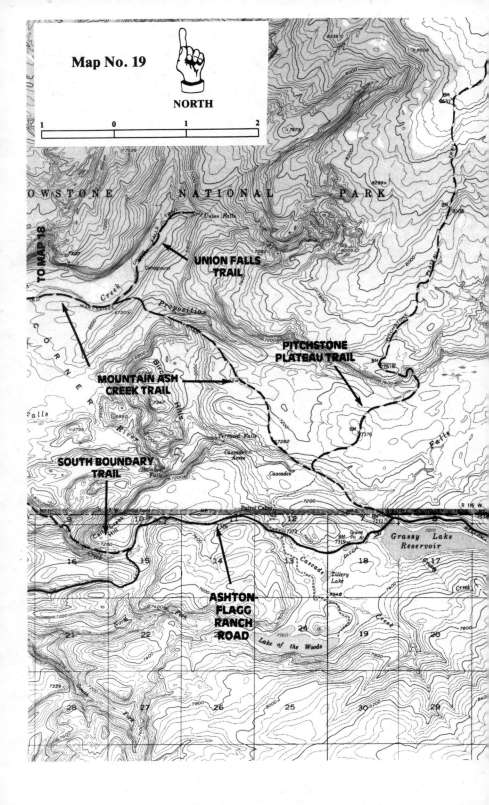

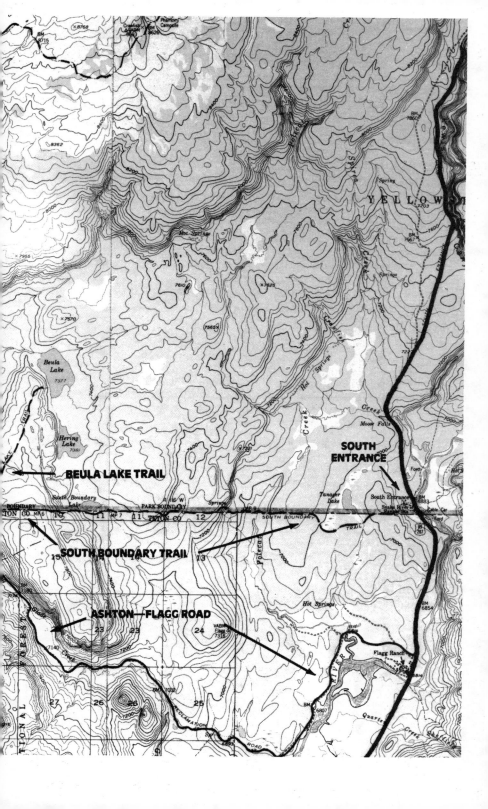

SOUTH BOUNDARY TRAIL
(Grassy Lake to South Entrance)

Grassy Lake to:

South Boundary Lake	2 miles	3 km
Polecat Creek	4	6.5
Tananger Lake	6	9.5
South Entrance	7	11

The best place to start this trail is the east end of Grassy Lake (on the Ashton-Flagg Road), the same trailhead as the Beula Lake Trail. Follow the Beula Lake Trail as it climbs up the forested ridge about ½ mile to the junction with the South Boundary Trail. The trail travels remarkably straight along the park's south boundary, through lodgepole pine, Engleman Spruce, and subalpine fir forest. The trail descends to the pond lily-lined shores of South Boundary Lake. From the lake the trail continues through forest to a good overlook of the Snake River valley and Huckleberry Ridge to the east. The trail descends steeply from the overlook to a bridge over Polecat Creek. It then climbs over a low ridge to Tananger Lake where moose may be seen, especially in the meadows north of the lake. The South Boundary Trail then descends and exits at the South Entrance N.P.S. horse corrals. *Map 19*

BEULA LAKE TRAIL
(3 miles, 5 kilometers)

The Beula Lake Trail starts from the eastern end of Grassy Lake Reservoir. Grassy Lake Reservoir is reached by taking the Ashton-Flagg Ranch Road (first left turn north of Flagg Ranch on Highway 89). The first section of this road is paved, but it soon turns to gravel and potholes.

The trail immediately climbs 400 feet up a steep forested ridge. Near the top, the South Boundary Trail crosses your path. The Beula Lake Trail remains on the top of this ridge about 1.5 miles and then descends gradually to the lodgepole-ringed shore of Beula Lake. In the past, trumpeter swans were seen on this lake. The Falls River flows out of the west end of Beula Lake. *Map 19*

Raven

SNAKE RIVER AREA

Here starts the Snake River; a river which will flow through Wyoming, Idaho, and Washington before it joins with the Columbia River to be carried into the Pacific Ocean. It's headwaters in Yellowstone contain a potpourri of interesting, beautiful, and wild scenery. Here you may observe elk feeding on the high meadows of Big Game Ridge; examine twisted, wind-shaped whitebark pine atop Mt. Sheridan; watch Rustic Geyser erupting on the shore of Heart Lake; or follow the Snake River as it flows through pristine meadows and marshes. But probably the most prominent feature of Yellowstone's Snake River Area is the burned trees. Throughout the 1980's, and especially during 1988, this area was hit by huge forest fires which left much of the area burned. As the saying goes, "Expect black trees and you won't be disappointed."

The area isn't for beginners; there are many stream and river crossings, long distances to be hiked and steep ridges to be climbed. But for those who do choose to hike here, the wilderness experience that can be gained is well worth the hardship. The best time to travel through the Snake River Area is during August and September when the streams, rivers and mosquitoes are on their ebb.

Yellowstone Lake and Mt. Sheridan.

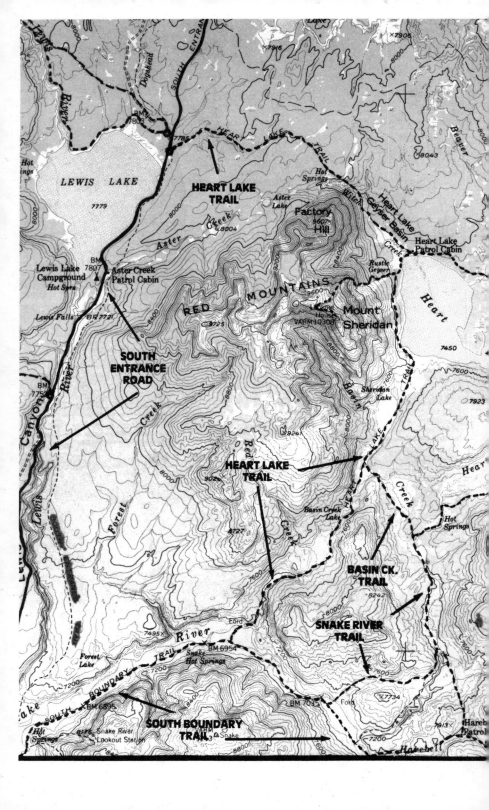

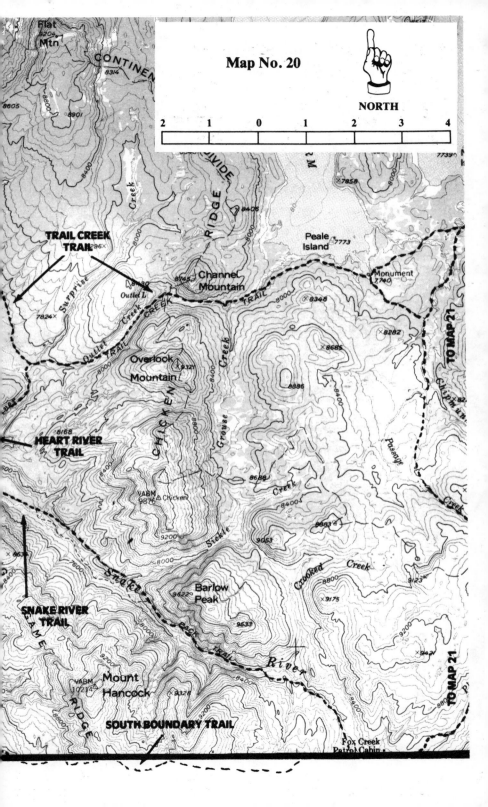

Map No. 20

NORTH

2 1 0 1 2 3 4

Flat Mtn
8204
CONTINEN
8314
8605
8800
8901

RIDGE
Creek
8406
7739

Peale Island 7773
7858
Monument 8740

TRAIL CREEK TRAIL
7296 ×
Surprise
Outlet L.
8765
Channel Mountain
TRAIL
8000
8348
8282
8685

7824 ×
Outlet Creek
CHICKEN CREEK TRAIL
Overlook Mountain
9321 ×
Grouse Creek
8400
8886

HEART RIVER TRAIL
8168
8800
Passage

8688
Creek
8400

VABM Chicken 9876
9200
Sickle
8683
9123

8000
9053
Crooked Creek
8800
9175
9200

SNAKE RIVER TRAIL
865 ×
Snake
7600
8000
Barlow Peak
9622
9533
River
8800
8400
942

Mount Hancock
VABM 10214
9200
3325 ×
RIDGE
9200
8400
8800

SOUTH BOUNDARY TRAIL
Fox Creek Patrol Cabin

TO MAP 21

TO MAP 21

The Heart Lake Trail travels from the Heart Lake Trailhead to the South Boundary Trail. Much of this area was burned during the 1988 fires. Heart Lake is the destination of many dayhikers and backpackers and thus receives relatively heavy use. The majority of people hiking the Heart Lake Trail start from the Heart Lake Trailhead, walk only as far as Heart Lake and return by the same route. For those wishing to travel the entire length of this trail it's best to travel north to south, as this avoids much of the altitude gain. Also, much of this area is good bear habitat, and it's not uncommon to see one here. *Map 20*

Heart Lake Trailhead (5.4 miles south of Grant Village on the South Entrance Road) to:

Heart Lake	8 miles	13 km
Mt. Sheridan Trail Jct.	8.7	14
Mt. Sheridan Lookout	12	19
Sheridan Lake	12	19
Basin Creek Lake	14.5	23
Snake River	18	30
South Entrance	23.5	38
Flagg Ranch	26.5	42.5

Starting at Heart Lake Trailhead, the first 5.5 miles of trail climbs very gradually through burned forest to an open thermal area where there is an impressive view, with Factory Hill and Heart Lake being the two most prominent features. From here the trail drops down steeply into the Witch Creek drainage, which contains a number of thermal features and provides dramatic steam clouds on cold clear mornings. The trail crosses Witch Creek on bridges, then meets the Trail Creek Trail at a junction near the shore of Heart Lake. The Heart Lake Trail heads southwest at this junction, and across another bridge over Witch Creek as it follows the shoreline of Heart Lake.

A few hundred yards down the trail you'll cross the run-off channels of Rustic Geyser and other thermal features located on the hillside to the west. (These thermal features can be reached by contouring over on a path that leaves the Heart Lake Trail near the Mt. Sheridan Trail junction. View these features from a safe distance; they are delicate and dangerous. By stepping in algae beds or on thin crust, you can wreck a fragile ecosystem and seriously burn yourself as well. The animal bones spread around the bottom of these pools are testimony to the hazard of hot water).

After crossing the run off channels, the Heart Lake Trail soon climbs up and away from the lake shore. In about ½ mile the trail meets the junction with the Mt. Sheridan Trail. The Heart Lake Trail continues on south of Heart Lake, passing Sheridan Lake and crossing Basin Creek. This area is a good place to spot migrating birds, such as grosbeaks, finches, sparrows, waterfowl, and hawks during the fall. Grizzly bears are active in this area during early summer, so stay alert. A short distance after crossing Basin Creek you'll come to a trail junction. (Here the Basin Creek Trail heads southeast to hook up to the Snake River Trail).

The Heart Lake Trail continues south up to Basin Creek Lake. After a short climb above this lake, the trail crosses a notch in the ridge and descends into the meadows of the Red Creek drainage. Red Creek is crossed about 2 miles from the notch, and another mile and a half brings you to the Snake River. Crossing the Snake River in this area shouldn't be tried before mid July, and after that it can still be thigh deep.

Once across the river, the Heart Lake Trail joins the South Boundary Trail. From this junction it's 5.5 miles to the next crossing of the Snake River at the South Entrance. This ford is deeper than the last, and can be over waist deep even after mid to late July. To avoid this ford, hike south approximately 3 miles; this involves climbing up a 200 foot ridge and contouring along that ridge as it parallels the Snake River. This will eventually lead you to the highway bridge over the Snake River, near Flagg Ranch.

MT. SHERIDAN LOOKOUT TRAIL
(3 miles, 5 kilometers)

The Mt. Sheridan trail climbs about 2,700 feet in 3 miles from its starting point on the Heart Lake Trail. The trail ends at a fire lookout station on top of the 10,308' peak where a ranger is stationed most of the summer to keep watch on forest fires. From the talus covered summit of Sheridan, you'll have a marvelous view of the Yellowstone Lake to the north, the Absaroka Range to the east, Pitchstone Plateau to the west, and the jagged peaks of the Teton Range to the south. The total distance from the Heart Lake Trailhead on the South Entrance Road to the summit of Mt. Sheridan is 12 miles, making this a popular two day-one night trip. If you plan to do it as a dayhike, make sure you're in good enough shape to get up and down before dark. Due to the bear activity, this is no place to be wandering around at night. *Map 20*

BASIN CREEK CUTOFF TRAIL
(2 miles, 3 kilometers)

The Basin Creek Trail follows Basin Creek, crossing it once, and connects the Heart Lake Trail with the Snake River Trail. Although only 2 miles long, it travels through some interesting meadows that are excellent places to spot a variety of bird and mammal life. Look for birds near the forest's edge and near the stream bank. You may also spot moose feeding in or near Basin Creek. Grizzlies frequent this area throughout the summer. *Map 20*

HEART RIVER TRAIL
(3 miles, 5 kilometers)

The Heart River Trail runs from the Trail Creek Trail (on the east end of Heart Lake) to the Snake River Trail. The trail follows Heart River through boggy areas and heavily burned forest. It makes two fords of the river which are knee to thigh deep after mid July. *Map 20*

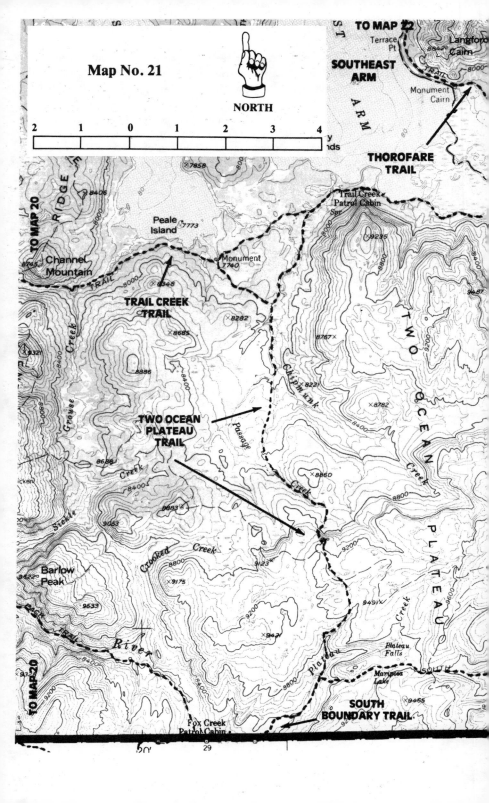

Map No. 21

NORTH

TO MAP 22

Terrace Pt

Langford Cairn

SOUTHEAST ARM

Monument Cairn

THOROFARE TRAIL

Trail Creek Patrol Cabin Spr

×9235

×9687

TO MAP 20

RIDGE

×7858

×8406

Peale Island ×7773

Channel Mountain

×8745

Monument 7740

×8348

TRAIL

TRAIL CREEK TRAIL

×8282

×8685

×9321

Grouse Creek

8886

×8767

×822

T W O

×8782

TWO OCEAN PLATEAU TRAIL

Passage

8686

Sickle

Creek

Chipmunk

Creek

O C E A N

×8860

Creek

9053

9683

×8660

Creek

Barlow Peak

9533

Crooked Creek

8800

×9175

×9123

9491×

P L A T E A U

Creek

River

×9421

9200

Plateau Falls

Mariposa Lake

Plateau

Creek

SOUTH

×9465

TO MAP 20

Fox Creek Patrol Cabin

SOUTH BOUNDARY TRAIL

29

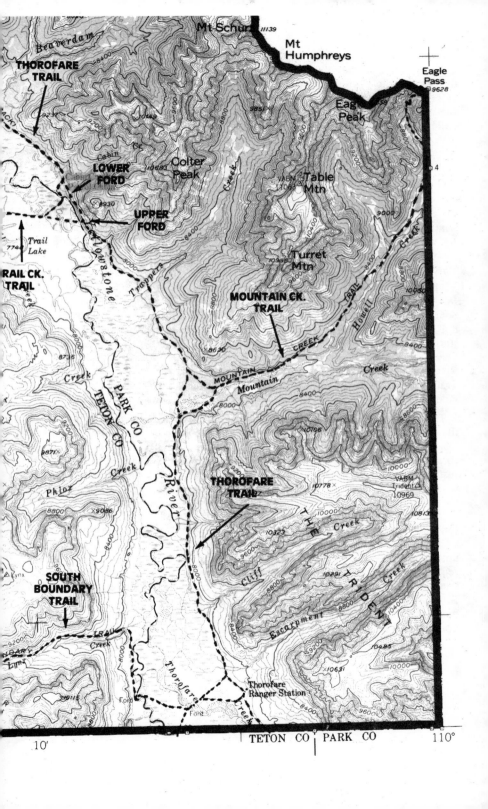

SOUTH BOUNDARY TRAIL

The South Boundary Trail travels from the South Entrance of Yellowstone to the Upper Yellowstone River Valley and Thorofare Ranger Station. For most of its 38 miles it parallels the park's south boundary, traveling along the Snake River, climbing over Big Game Ridge and Two Ocean Plateau, and finally crossing the Yellowstone and Thorofare Rivers. The variety of scenery is fascinating, including many miles of burned forest, but the hiking and stream crossings can be strenuous. The description of the South Boundary Trail will be divided into three sections: 1) South Entrance to Harebell Patrol Cabin, 2) Harebell Patrol Cabin to Fox Creek Patrol Cabin, and 3) Fox Creek Cabin to Thorofare Ranger Station.

SOUTH ENTRANCE TO HAREBELL CABIN

South Entrance to:

Jct. with Heart Lake Trail	5.5 miles	9 km
Jct. with Snake River Cutoff	8	13
Harebell Patrol Cabin	12	19

There are actually two starting points for the South Boundary Trail along the south Entrance Road. One is located at the trailhead about 200 yards south of the South Entrance Station. This requires a deep crossing of the Snake River, usually not fordable until mid to late July, and thigh to waist deep after that. The other starting point is on the south side of the highway bridge over the Snake River at Flagg Ranch (3 miles south of South Entrance). This route parallels the Snake River upstream on the hillside to the east, then descends to the South Boundary Trail in the meadows across from the South Entrance Station. This route adds 3 miles to the distances listed above.

The South Boundary Trail follows the Snake River, mainly through forest, to the Snake Hot Springs, which are a small group of interesting thermal features located along the bank of the river. (During the winter, the runoff from these springs keeps the Snake from freezing immediately downstream of this area. Yet just upstream, at the Heart Lake Trail ford, the river will usually be solid enough to ski across). At 5.5 miles the junction with the Heart Lake Trail is reached. From the junction, the South Boundary trail turns southeast through burned forest until it reaches a long meadow. At the north end of the meadow you will arrive at the junction with the Snake River Cutoff Trail. The South Boundary Trail continues to the southern end of the meadow, then leaves the Snake River and heads upstream on Wolverine Creek. The trail soon crosses Wolverine Creek, which requires a knee deep ford (not fordable early in the season), and then comes to another trail junction. (The trail heading south follows Wolverine Creek into the Bridger-Teton National Forest). From the junction, the South Boundary Trail heads east and climbs 400 vertical feet in the next 1.5 mile and tops out on a ridge above Harebell Creek. Harebell Patrol Cabin is a mile further. *Map 20*

HAREBELL CABIN TO FOX CREEK CABIN
(11.5 miles, 18.5 kilometers)

From the Harebell Cabin the trail follows Harebell Creek up the slopes of Big Game Ridge through heavily burned forest. Harebell Creek is crossed twice in this section. Once out of the trees, you'll climb through alpine meadows to the high point of the ridge (10,065'). You will have climbed about 2,400' in 7 miles from the cabin. On a clear day the view from Big Game Ridge is well worth the climb. You can see Wyoming's two highest mountain ranges, the Teton Range to the southwest and the Wind River Range to the southeast. And with a name like Big Game Ridge, it's only fitting that you'll probably also spot some elk. The elk feed on the grasses and forbs here from July through October. The descent from Big Game Ridge is steep, but enjoyable, as it passes through open stands of whitebark pine. Grizzlies feed on the pine nuts in this area during the fall, so stay alert. Once down off the ridge, you'll come to the meadows of the Snake River. On the west side of the river you will come to a junction with the Snake River Trail. The South Boundary Trail continues east across the river (an easy knee-deep crossing after mid summer) to Fox Creek Patrol Cabin. (There is a trail heading south from the cabin area that goes into Bridger Teton National Forest and leads to the actual headwaters of the Snake River and an extensive Forest Service trail system). *Maps 20, 21*

FOX CREEK PATROL CABIN TO THOROFARE RANGER STATION
(Lynx Creek Trail)

Fox Creek Cabin to:		
Jct. with Two Ocean Plateau Trail	3 miles	5 km
Mariposa Lake	4	6.5
Continental Divide	5.5	9
Yellowstone River ford	11.5	18.5
Thorofare Ranger Station	14	22

From Fox Creek Patrol Cabin the South Boundary Trail travels up Plateau Creek, crossing it once, through intermittently burned forest. The trail crosses Mariposa Creek then immediately comes to a junction with the Two Ocean Plateau Trail. The South Boundary trail continues east up Mariposa Creek to Mariposa Lake. The trail has gained about 900 feet from the cabin to Mariposa Lake. Mariposa is a shallow lake, which contains cutthroat trout and is surrounded by meadows. East of the lake you make a shallow crossing of Mariposa Creek and continue up another 300 vertical feet through wet meadows and whitebark pine forest to the crest of Two Ocean Plateau (approx. elevation: 9,300'). Here you cross the Continental Divide and descend into the drainage of the Atlantic Ocean.

The meadows of the Two Ocean Plateau are one of the highlights of this trail. Eagles, elk, moose, and bear all frequent this area throughout the summer and fall. Wild flowers abound. As you continue east down into the Lynx Creek side of the divide there will be spectacular views of the Yellowstone River Valley and the Trident Mountain to the east. (As of spring 1990, the section of trail along Lynx Creek makes four crossings of the creek and slogs through hundreds of yards of bogs and wet meadows. It is scheduled to be rerouted or improved in the next few years.) Once the trail reaches the Yellowstone River Valley you will have descended about 1400 feet in the approximately 4.5 miles from the divide. *Map 21*

The trail now parallels the Yellowstone River through burned forest for about 1.5 miles until it reaches the Yellowstone River ford. This is a deep ford (waist deep) even in late season. Luckily the river flows fairly slowly through this section. From the ford the trail turns east and out into the meadows of the Yellowstone River Valley. From these meadows you see mountains in all directions. It's a very special spot and a long way from the nearest road. About a mile from the Yellowstone ford, the trail comes to a junction. (The trail to Bridger Lake heads south from here). A short distance further on the South Boundary Trail you will reach the ford of the Thorofare River. This is also a deep ford, but by scouting up or downstream a short ways you can usually find a shallower place to cross (thigh to waist deep after early August). Once you get to the east side of the ford keep your wading shoes on because the trail soon crosses another small side channel of the Thorofare River.

About ¼ mile east of the Thorofare Ford, the South Boundary Trail comes to a junction with a spur trail (which leads ¾ mile northeast to the Thorofare Trail. If your destination is somewhere north on the Thorofare Trail, Yellowstone Lake, East Entrance Road, etc., this spur is the trail you want to take). Continuing east on the South Boundary Trail you will reach the Thorofare Ranger Station, which has a ranger living there most of the summer and fall. From a trail junction out in front of the pasture fence at the ranger station, you can either travel north on the Thorofare Trail, or south to the Bridger Teton National Forest and an extensive network of trails.

SNAKE RIVER TRAIL

Snake River Cutoff Junction to:

Jct. with trail from Harebell cabin	2.5 miles	4 km
Basin Creek Cutoff Trail	4.5	7.2
Heart River Trail Jct.	7	11
Fox Creek Patrol Cabin	18	30

This wild, seldom hiked trail follows the Snake River through a variety of interesting terrain, including an 11 mile stretch through a scenic canyon. Moose, deer, and elk are all frequently seen here. The trail starts at the junction of the South Boundary Trail (8 miles east of the South Entrance) and the Snake River Cutoff Trail. Follow the Snake River Cutoff for the first 2.5 miles until you reach the actual Snake River Trail. Thanks to a major reroute the Snake River Trail now *only* crosses the Snake River four times in 18 miles. The first ford, and furthest downstream, is the deepest—usually thigh deep after late July. The Snake River Trail ends at its junction with the South Boundary Trail near Fox Creek Patrol Cabin. Much of the area around this trail was burned during the fires of 1988. *Maps 20, 21.*

Southeast Arm and Colter Peak. Photo by Mike Lavigna.

THE THOROFARE AREA

The Thorofare Area has a lot of hiking potential. With hikes ranging in distance from 4 miles to over 50 miles, it contains a vast amount of honest-to-goodness breathtaking scenery. The remote arms of Yellowstone Lake, the wild marshes and meadows of the Upper Yellowstone River, and the snowy summits of Yellowstone's highest peaks are all contained in this area. To reach these spots you've got to do some long hiking, wade some cold streams and swat a few mosquitoes. To help you decide whether to brave the hardships, some of the area's interesting features are described below.

Yellowstone Lake is quite a place. It's over 20 miles long, 14 miles wide, over 300 feet deep, and its clear water is always cold. Native cutthroat trout thrive in the cold clear water, feeding on invertebrates, shiner minnows and each other. The cutthroat is a vital element in the lake area's food chain. Yellowstone's pelicans alone eat an estimated 40,000 cutthroat a year. The trout are also eaten by otter, mink, mergansers, cormorants, gulls, osprey, eagles and even grizzly bears. The grizzlies snatch their fish when the trout swim up the small steams to spawn from May to July. The South and Southeast Arms of Yellowstone Lake are good areas to see all of these fish-eating animals. Osprey and bald eagles nest in the trees along the shoreline, especially on secluded Frank Island, and can often be seen flying out over the lake in search of food. Gulls, cormorants and pelicans nest on the Molly Islands in the Southeast Arm. You might see the pelicans skimming low and fast above the water as they look for a reachable trout.

Into the Southeast Arm flows the Upper Yellowstone River; the remote marsh, meadow and forested valley, through which this river meanders, is seen by few of the park's 2 million yearly visitors. Its gravelly banks and lush marshes are home for spotted sandpipers, snipes, sandhill cranes, great blue herons, Canada geese and a wide variety of ducks. Moose may be seen just about anywhere at anytime in the valley, and elk may be seen feeding in the meadows early or late in the day.

This area has long been used as route of travel by the Indians, trappers and explorers of the region. Artifacts left by the native people lead us to believe that the area has been travelled by humans for at least the last 8,000 years. There are still old tepee rings and lean-to's visible to the discerning eye in spots that would make beautiful campsites even today. Long before anyone had heard of ripstop nylon, aluminum pack frames, or freeze-dried ice cream, people had used the area as a thoroughfare between Jackson's Hole and points north; they would travel over Two Ocean Pass, down into the Upper Yellowstone Valley and then north along Yellowstone Lake, where they would then branch off in many directions. The names in this area remain as a reminder of these early travellers: Trapper's Creek, Colter Peak (named for John Colter who was probably the first white man to visit Yellowstone), Bridger Lake (named for Jim Bridger, famous mountain man and scout) and the Absaroka Range (named for the Absaroka, or Crow, Indians, who hunted this area during the summers). The scenery is just as they left it, even the burned areas.

Burned areas have been part of the scenery here as long as there have been forests; and the 1990's are no different. Much of the Thorofare Area was burned, to varying degrees, during the fires of 1988. If you hike through the burned sections, you'll find that the recent fires have added an extra dimension of interest to an already fascinating region.

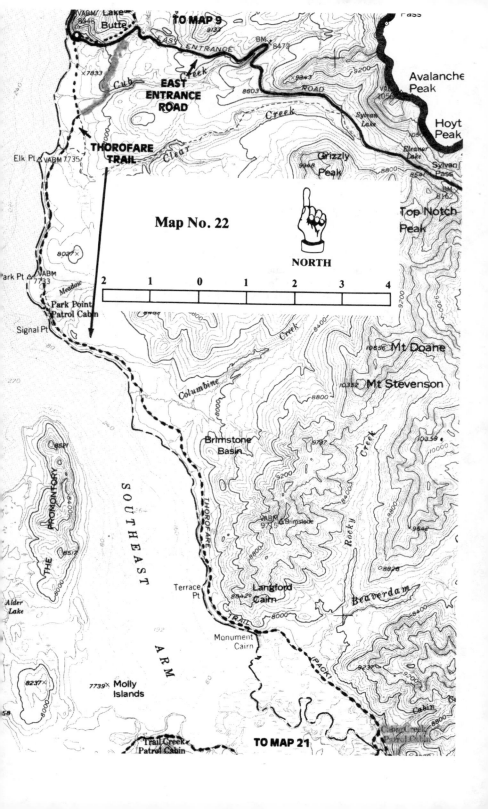

TO MAP 9

EAST
ENTRANCE
ROAD

THOROFARE
TRAIL

Map No. 22

NORTH

2   1   0   1   2   3   4

Avalanche Peak

Hoyt Peak

Grizzly Peak

Sylvan Pass

Top Notch Peak

Elk Pt △ VABM 7735

Park Pt △ VABM 7733

Park Point Patrol Cabin

Signal Pt

THE PROMONTORY

Alder Lake

Mt Doane

Mt Stevenson

Brimstone Basin

VABM 9715 △ Brimstone

SOUTHEAST

Rocky Creek

Beaverdam

Columbine Creek

THOROFARE TRAIL

Terrace Pt

Langford Cairn

Monument Cairn

(PACK)

ARM

Molly Islands

Cabin

Cabin Creek Patrol Cabin

Trail Creek Patrol Cabin

TO MAP 21

From 9-Mile Trailhead (approximately 9 miles from Fishing Bridge Junction on the East Entrance Road) to:

	3 miles	5 km
Clear Creek	3 miles	5 km
Park Point Cabin	6.5	10.5
Columbine Creek	9	14.5
Terrace Point	15.5	25
Lower Ford Jct.	19.5	31
Upper Ford Jct.	20.5	33
Mountain Ck. Trail Jct.	24.5	39
Mtn. Ck. Trail Jct. (south)	26	41.5
South Boundary Trail Jct.	31	49.5
Thorofare Ranger Station	32	51
Bridger Lake	34	54.5

The Thorofare Trailhead is located about 9 miles east of Fishing Bridge on the East Entrance Road (just west of the entrance to the Lake Butte Drive). From the trailhead the trail travels through level forest for about 1.5 miles to Cub Creek. Both Cub Creek and Clear Creek can have high swift water early in the season, but can usually be crossed on fallen logs. Cub and Clear Creek are also both frequented by grizzly bears during the early season spawn. With the grizzlies intent on fishing for trout, the roar of the creek, and the dense forest, it is very easy to surprise a bear here. In recent years there have been restrictions on travel in this area during spawning season; so check at a ranger station for current information before you plan on hiking this area. From Clear Creek the trail travels through dense forest to Park Point. Just before reaching Park Point Cabin the trail runs along the edge of a meadow where there is a good view of Mt. Doane and Mt. Stevenson. From Park Point beach you can see Dot and Frank Islands, The Promontory and the South and Southeast Arms of the lake. As you might guess, watching the sunset across Yellowstone Lake from Park Point is a memorable experience. After crossing Meadow Creek, which is usually slow and shallow, the trail continues to travel through the woods, away from the shoreline. About ½ mile south of Meadow Creek the trail travels for about a mile through an open grass and sage bench above the lake. Columbine Creek is about 2 miles further and can be crossed on logs after water levels go down in mid July.

From Columbine Creek to Terrace Point the Thorofare Trail is in the trees with no views of the lake, mountains or meadows. If you're one of the people that bemoaned the loss of trees during the fires of 1988, and have an affinity for thick lodgepole pine forest, then you'll love this section of trail.

At Terrace Point the trail goes through a series of meadows where there is a fantastic panoramic view of the valley of the upper Yellowstone River, with Colter Peak to the east and Two Ocean Plateau on the west side of the valley. (To get an even better view, walk up the open slopes above the trail for about ¼ mile). The Thorofare Trail continues through the meadows of Beaverdam Creek, a short distance further, where elk, moose, and sandhill cranes are often seen. Grizzly bears also spend a lot of time in these meadows, but aren't usually seen. The ford of Beaverdam Creek is knee deep after late July and can be impassable on foot before mid July. After crossing Beaverdam Creek, the trail winds through open meadows and a stretch of thick willows. It's difficult to see very far in front of you here; so make noise. No sense surprising a bear if you don't have to. About a mile south of Beaverdam Creek, you'll encounter the first of the burned trees. From this point south, most of the forest along the way was burned to varying degrees by the fires of 1988.

At 19.5 miles the junction with the Trail Creek Trail (to Heart Lake) is met. This junction is called the Lower Ford Junction because it leads to the Lower Ford of the Yellowstone River. One mile south of this junction is another junction with the Trail Creek Trail. This one is called the Upper Ford Junction and, of course, leads to the Upper Ford of the Yellowstone River. Continuing south on the Thorofare Trail you'll cross Trapper's Creek (knee deep after mid July) and go through burned forest to Turret View meadows. Here is an impressive full frontal view of Turret Mountain. About 1.5 miles south of Trappers Creek you'll travel through another big meadow which provides a good view of the Trident to the south.

At 24.5 miles the Thorofare Trail meets the Mountain Creek Trail junction. (The Mountain Creek Trail leads to Eagle Pass). About one mile south of the junction, the Thorofare Trail crosses Mountain Creek (knee deep after late July) and continues to the southern junction with the Mountain Creek Trail. The next 6 miles of the Thorofare Trail are quite scenic as it travels through meadows and forest and, in some places, along the Yellowstone River. There are good views of the walls of the Trident directly above you to the east and of Two Ocean Plateau across the valley to the west. About a mile north of Thorofare Ranger Station the trail reaches the junction with the South Boundary Trail. (Go right—southwest—at this junction to reach the South Boundary/Lynx Creek Trail and the South Entrance). Go left—southeast—to reach Thorofare Ranger Station and the Thorofare River Trail outside of the park. You can reach Bridger Lake and Two Ocean Pass, in Bridger Teton National Forest, by either route.

Veering left at this junction, The Thorofare Trail continues another 1.5 mile south, past Thorofare Ranger Station, to the park boundary. (Just before the boundary, there is a turnoff for Bridger Lake). The Thorofare ranger claims that this is one of the most remote spots in the lower 48 states, being 32 miles from the nearest road of any kind. The Thorofare Trail continues outside of Yellowstone Park and can be followed another 18 miles up to Deer Creek Pass, and then down into the South Fork of the Shoshone River. That is only one of numerous possibilities for long trips in this remote area. *Maps 21, 22*

TWO OCEAN PLATEAU TRAIL

Junction with Trail Creek Trail to:

South Boundary Trail	12.5 miles	20 km
Mariposa Lake	13.5	22
Fox Creek Patrol Cabin	15.5	25

The Two Ocean Plateau Trail connects the Trail Creek Trail with the South Boundary Trail as it travels up and over the plateau and the Continental Divide. The high meadows of Two Ocean Plateau are the summer home for herds of elk that migrate up from their wintering grounds in Jackson Hole. By migrating from lower to higher elevations, the elk are following the growing season for plants as

149

the season progresses up the hillsides. This way the elk arrive just in time for the new tender sprouts of plant growth. By moving to these higher, cooler, and windier places the elk also escape the biting insects. The Two Ocean Plateau received its name because its streams flow into both the Atlantic and Pacific drainages.

The Two Ocean Plateau Trail receives little use, so expect the tread on the trail to be light in places. A topographic map is a must here. Starting from the Trail Creek Trail (1.5 miles west of Trail Creek Cabin) the Two Ocean Plateau Trail follows Chipmunk Creek and its meadows, crossing the creek once, up to the confluence of Chipmunk Creek and Passage Creek. After a shallow crossing of Passage Creek, the trail climbs about 800 feet in 4 miles to the Continental Divide. Trail work in this area has eliminated 5 crossings of Passage Creek (trail will be shown incorrectly on pre-1978 topo maps). Much of the Two Ocean Plateau was burned in the 1988 fires, as will be evident from the trail. After crossing the divide, the trail descends 700 vertical feet along a fork of Plateau Creek and joins the South Boundary Trail. From this point Mariposa Lake is 1 mile to the east. *Maps 20, 21*

MOUNTAIN CREEK TRAIL
(May be referred to as Monument Creek Trail on some older maps)

The Mountain Creek Trail travels from the Thorofare Trail up through a beautiful mountain valley to Eagle Pass. The upper section of the trail is especially scenic as it provides prolonged views of Yellowstone's highest peaks. Elk can be seen in these upper meadows and bear and moose are spotted along the lower stretch of trail. Most of the forest along this trail was burned in the fires of 1988. This is also the route of choice for those attempting to climb Eagle Peak. This peak is not a simple scramble and has turned back and injured it's share of mountaineers. Check at Lake Ranger Station before attempting this climb. *Map 21*

Junction with Thorofare Trail (24.5 miles south of the East Entrance Road) to:

Dike Creek Trail Jct.		
Eagle Pass	6.5 miles	10.5 km
Eagle Creek Campground on the	10	16.5
North Fork Highway	28.5	45.5

The Mountain Creek Trail leaves the Thorofare Trail from two different junctions, about a mile apart. Starting from the northern junction, the Mountain Creek Trail heads east through fairly level terrain. After about a mile the trail passes the junction with the southern spur back to the Thorofare Trail. The Mountain Creek Trail now follows east along Mountain Creek where there are good views of the Trident to the south. Soon the trail leads uphill away from Mountain Creek and into the burned forest. For the next 3 miles you'll travel through the burn, crossing many small creeks. Turret and Table Mountains are right above you to the north. The trail then descends down to the meadows of Howell Creek, crosses an unnamed side creek (that must be waded), and eventually passes the Dike Creek Trail junction. (The Dike Creek Trail climbs up into Bridger-Teton National Forest and over a short pass back to the upper reaches of Mountain Creek). The trail is maintained only a short way past the park boundary.

From the Dike Creek Trail Junction, the Mountain Creek Trail continues past the Howell Creek Patrol Cabin and through more burned forest. About a mile past the cabin the trail starts climbing and will gain about 1,000 feet in the next 2 miles up to Eagle Pass. The sheer walls of Eagle Peak fill the view to the northwest, and Pinnacle Mountain (100 feet higher than Eagle Peak) is above the trail to the northeast. Eagle Pass is a very special place. You can see a long way in every direction and everything you see is wild country.

From the pass, the North Fork Highway to Cody is about 18.5 miles away via the Eagle Creek Trail. The first 5 miles are very steep; and as of 1989, the entire eighteen miles was in poor condition and unpleasant to hike. The trail ends at the Shoshone River where there are some summer cabins. Veer left on the trail past these cabins and you'll arrive at a suspension bridge after 0.3 mile. This bridge will take you to Eagle Creek Campground. If you don't turn left past these cabins you will remain on the Eagle Creek Trail. This will veer right (east) and end up a mile downstream at Eagle Creek Trailhead. This route requires a deep, fast ford of the Shoshone River. Check at the U.S.F.S. Ranger Station at Wapiti for current conditions on the Eagle Creek Trail.

TRAIL CREEK TRAIL

The Trail Creek Trail connects the Heart Lake Trail with the Thorofare Trail. Along its 22 mile length it provides access to Outlet Lake, The South and Southeast Arms of Yellowstone Lake, Two Ocean Plateau Trail and the Upper Yellowstone River. The variety of scenery and wildlife along this trail makes it one of the more interesting hiking routes in the park. The trail is mainly level, with only one low pass to cross. Most of the forest along this trail was burned in the fires of 1988.

From Heart Lake Ranger Station to:

Heart River Trail	4 miles	6.5 km
Outlet Lake	7	11
Two Ocean Plateau Trail	13	21
East Jct. with Two Ocean Trail	15.5	25
Trail Creek Cabin	17	27
Yellowstone River Ford Jct.	21.5	34.5
Thorofare Trail	22	35

From Heart Lake Ranger Station, the Trail Creek Trail travels east down the shoreline of Heart Lake for a few hundred yards and then turns up and away from the lake. The trail soon crosses Beaver Creek and its marshy meadows. Continuing through the forest, the Trail Creek Trail passes the junction with the Heart River Trail, then crosses Surprise Creek and begins climbing up the drainage of Outlet Creek. The trail crosses Outlet Creek in a long meadow, then follows the creek to the north end of the meadows. The trail leaves Outlet Creek, heads east into the forest, and begins climbing up to the Continental Divide. The divide is at about 8,000', which is only 500' higher than Heart Lake. Geologist's believe that at one time Yellowstone Lake may have flowed into the Snake River/Pacific Ocean drainage instead of its present day Yellowstone River/Atlantic Ocean drainage. They think that the way you just came may have been the route that water leaving the lake took, as it flowed into the Snake River.

From the divide, you will descend gradually through the meadows of Grouse Creek. Grouse Creek, along with most of the other creeks flowing into Yellowstone Lake, is filled with spawning cutthroat trout from late June through mid July. As you might guess, this easy source of fresh meat attracts grizzly bears; and this entire area south of Yellowstone Lake becomes a hot bed of bear activity early in the summer (hiking may be restricted in this area during spawning season). About 2 miles from the divide the trail leaves Grouse Creek and heads into the forest where it parallels the South Arm of Yellowstone Lake. The Trail Creek Trail meets the Two Ocean Plateau Trail near a finger of the South Arm. This area is a haven for waterfowl and moose throughout the summer. The Trail Creek Trail continues another 2.5 miles through forest, meadow, and across Chipmunk Creek (calf deep after midsummer) to another junction with the Two Ocean Plateau Trail.

From the Two Ocean Jct., the trail travels through meadows and burned forest for another 1.5 miles until you come to the Trail Creek Cabin bypass junction. At this junction the trail to the left leads to the lake shore and Trail Creek Patrol Cabin, a few hundred yards away. The Trail Creek cabin area contains a National Park Service cabin, barn, corral, pasture, and boat dock to support the backcountry patrol operations. Walking past all this human development 25 miles from the nearest road can nudge you out of your wilderness state of mind. So unless you want to talk with the ranger, you should continue on the Trail Creek Trail which turns to the right. After about ¼ mile on this trail you'll come to a similar junction on the other side of the cabin area. Then the Trail Creek Trail continues east following the shoreline for the next ½ mile or so. Leaving the lake shore, the trail follows the meadows of Trail Creek, which are filled with migrating waterfowl and elk in the fall. The trail makes some log crossings of spring creeks in this area. Then Trail Creek is crossed by bridge. It is possible to reach Trail Lake at this point by following Trail Creek upstream along an unmaintained trail.

From the Trail Creek Bridge you will continue east through forest burned in the 1988 fires. After about .2 mile the trail enters an area of forest that was burned in 1974 and then reburned in 1988. The transition is subtle, but noticeable. Thanks to the fires, there are now good views of Colter Peak to the east. In the past the old trail to Trail Lake left from this area, but was destroyed in the fires. Check at Lake Ranger Station for the current status on this trail.

About ½ mile west of the Yellowstone River the Trail Creek Trail splits. The trail to the left (north) goes to the Lower Ford of the Yellowstone River and the north portion of the Thorofare Trail. The trail to the right (south) goes to the Upper Ford and the southern portion of the Thorofare Trail. One ford is usually easier than the other; but it changes from year to year. Thus the Lower Ford might be passable while the Upper Ford is not, or vice versa. Also, during 1989, this crossing fluctuated very rapidly after heavy rainfalls. This may be a result of lack of ground cover in the watershed due to the fires of 1988. If so, I would guess it will stabilize as the ground cover returns. With the exception of periods of heavy rain, both crossings are usually passable (thigh to waist deep) by early August. Both fords are marked with orange markers that show the shallowest spot to cross. After crossing at either ford, the Trail Creek Trail will meet the Thorofare Trail after a short climb through the forest. *Maps 20, 21*

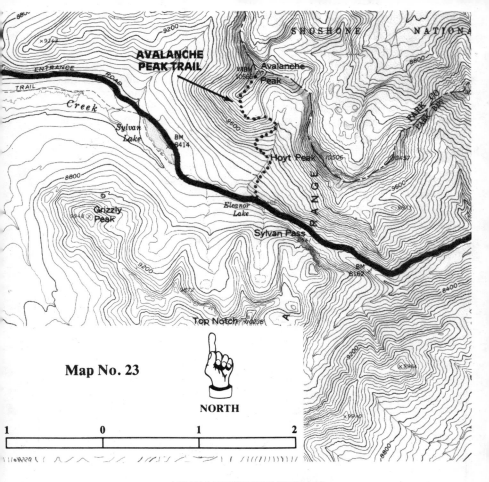

AVALANCHE PEAK TRAIL
(2 miles, 3 kilometers)

This steep trail climbs 2,100 vertical feet in 2 miles to the summit of 10,566' Avalanche Peak. The view from the top is one of the most impressive in the park. The trail is unmarked, but the tread work and drainage were improved by a Sierra Club work crew in 1988. The trail is now easily navigated; although it still remains steeper than most park trails. Good traction soles on your shoes are a must. Expect snow on the trail before mid July. The trail starts at the picnic area at the west end of Eleanor Lake (2 miles east of Sylvan Lake on the East Entrance Road). Across the highway (north) from the picnic area is a stream running down the hillside. the trail starts to the right of the stream and begins climbing steeply through the forest. About ½ mile up, the trail crosses the stream. Do not take the trail that goes directly up the drainage; this route is steeper and the N.P.S. is trying to rehabilitate it. From the stream, the trail traverses west a few hundred yards out into an old avalanche slide. Notice the trees in various stages of regrowth from the periodical avalanches. A few hundred yards further the trail traverses back east into the mature whitebark pine forest.

About a mile from the trailhead, the trail finally comes out of the trees at the bottom of the Southeast Bowl of Avalanche Peak. You will be able to see the summit from this point. Now the trail again turns to the west and begins climbing up a steep scree slope. This will eventually take you up to the shoulder of the south ridge, and from this point there are a number of paths up the remaining scree slope to the summit ridge. Depending upon where you gain the summit ridge, the true summit will be a few hundred yards away along the ridge top to the northeast. From the summit it is possible to drop straight down a steep trail to the northeast and loop back to the Southeast Bowl. This trail is not marked or maintained.

You may want to take a National Park Service Ranger-Naturalist led group hike up Avalanche Peak. These are offered frequently throughout the summer. The ranger will be able to provide a good insight to Yellowstone's alpine ecology, and will also be able to help you identify landmarks that are visible in that incredible panorama from the summit. Check at any park visitor center for more information. *Map 23*

Osprey

APPENDIX

GRIZZLY BEARS

Sources of Information:

GRIZZLY BEAR COMPENDIUM 1987
Sponsored by the Interagency Grizzly Bear Committee. Produced by the
National Wildlife Federation, Washington, D.C.
—This is the source for any scientific information on grizzlies. It covers
research findings on behavior, feeding, human-bear relationships, mortality
factors, and management considerations. The book also contains a compre-
hensive bibliography on grizzly studies.

Stephen Herrero, BEAR ATTACKS, THEIR CAUSES AND AVOIDANCE
(New York: Nick Lyons Books, 1985).
—Required reading for anyone who does much hiking in bear country.
Besides attacks, it also covers bear behavior and management.

Paul Schullery, THE BEARS OF YELLOWSTONE
(Boulder: Roberts Rinehart, Inc., 1986).
—This book offers a broad range of information about Yellowstone's bears,
with especially good information on the history of management.

Sources for Capsaicin Bear Repellents:

Bushwacker Backpack & Supply Co. Inc.
P.O. Box 4721
Missoula, MT 59806   (406) 728-6241

Bongard Protection Systems
10850 S.W. 113th Place
Miami, FL 33126

Animal Repellents, Inc.
Griffin, GA 30223

General Information Books About Backcountry Hiking:

John Hart, WALKING SOFTLY IN THE WILDERNESS.
(San Francisco: Sierra Club Books, 1984).

Marlyn Doan, HIKING LIGHT.
(Seattle: the Mountaineers, 1982).

Water Treatment

S. Erlander and E. Meyer, GIARDIA AND GIARDIASIS.
(New York: Plenum Press, 1984).
—A collection of scientific papers concerning everything from morphology to pathology to transmission mechanisms of Giardia.

Kenneth Iserson, MD, WILDERNESS MEDICAL
SOCIETY—POSITION STATEMENTS 1989. (P.O. Box
397, Point Reyes Station, CA 94956)
—This is a very thorough source on water treatment methods, as well as on all aspects of advanced medical care in the backcountry.

Sources for Topographic Maps around Yellowstone National Park

Cody, Wyoming:

Sunlight Sports
1323 Sheridan Ave.
(307) 587-9517

New Post Office Store
1121 13th St.
(307) 587-9517

Jackson, Wyoming:

Teton Mountaineering
86 East Broadway
(307) 733-3595

Skinny Skis, Inc.
65 West Deloney St.
(307) 733-6094

West Yellowstone, MT:

Bud Lilly's Trout Shop
39 Madison Ave.
(406) 646-7801

Eagle's Store
3 Canyon Street
(406) 838-2234

Gardiner, MT:

Parks Fly Shop
(406) 848-7314

Cooke City, MT:

Cooke City Store
(406) 838-2234

Also available in Yellowstone National Park at:

Old Faithful Visitor Center

To order by mail:

Map Distribution
U.S. Geologic Survey
Building 41
Box 25286, Federal Center
Denver, CO 80225

For more information: Books, Field Guides, Maps on Yellowstone National Park.

- *Plants of Yellowstone and Grand Teton National Parks,* by Richard Shaw

- *Field Guide to Rocky Mountain Wildflowers,* by F. Craighead, J. Craighead and R. Davis

- *Birds of Yellowstone,* by Terry McEneaney

- *Yellowstone and Fires of Change,* by George Weurthner

- *Yellowstone on Fire,* by Robert Ekey

- *Field Guide to the Mammals,* by W. Burt and R. Grossenheider

- *The Yellowstone Story, Vol. I and II,* by Aubrey Haines (History)

- *Hiking Maps of Yellowstone,* by Trails Illustrated

All available from Yellowstone Association, Box 117, Yellowstone National Park, WY 82190 (307-344-7381 ext. 2349)

Avocet

INDEX

ACKNOWLEDGEMENTS

As much as I'd like to think I know enough about Yellowstone's backcountry to write a trail guide by myself, I'm afraid I'm going to have to admit that this book incorporates the knowledge and experience of many people. First, there were numerous backcountry rangers, past and present, who provided initial information for the book and revisions for the current edition. They are Rick McAdam, Terry Danforth, Randy King, Joe Fowler, Mark McCutcheon, Rick Bennett, Steve Anderson, Doug Ridley, Bundy Phillips, John Litherland, Mike Ross, Andrew Mitchell, Dunbar Susong, Bob Flather, Marv Miller, Scott Powers, Gerald Mernin, and Tim Blank. The above group has put in a lot of years and miles in Yellowstone's backcountry and I feel fortunate that they shared their knowledge for this book. Thanks to Jean Nuetzel and Laura Bittner for researching the information on the backcountry deaths, and to Melissa McAdam for her help with the maps and map information in this book. Sandy Fowler, of the National Park Service Backcountry Office, and Kathi Noaker reviewed the text and offered thoughtful advice on the contents. The Yellowstone Association has continued to support the book and has done everything possible to keep the book's price low. And finally thanks to Dave Phillips and Bob Jackson, long time Thorofare Rangers, who patiently taught me about being a backcountry ranger and bestowed upon me some of their abundance of backcountry lore.

With the help of the people I've mentioned, every effort has been made to eliminate mistakes from *Yellowstone Trails*. But if you find something in this book that you feel is wrong, misleading, or confusing I want to know. If it is appropriate I will change it in the next edition of the guide. Please send your comments to: Mark Marschall c/o Yellowstone Association, Box 117, Yellowstone National Park, WY 82190.

Yellowstone's beauty can disguise the inherent dangers of travelling in the backcountry. The following people were killed while on backcountry trips in Yellowstone between 1980 and 1990. Let this list instill caution in the rest of us and hopefully prevent further tragedies.

1980—Duane McClure, *park ranger, drowned while doing canoe patrol on Yellowstone Lake.*

1982—James Wilkerson, *drowned while fording Hellroaring Creek.*

1984—Brigitta Fredenhagen, *killed by a grizzly bear at White Lake.*

1985—Leroy Stuppy, *drowned in Yellowstone River while fishing near Hellroaring Bridge.*

1985—Albert Paul Knight, *fell while climbing on Cutoff Mountain.*

1985—Kent Rich, *fell while climbing on The Thunderer.*

1985—Keith Marsh, *died from mistakenly eating water hemlock at Heart Lake.*

1988—John Mark Williams, *fell into a hot spring at Shoshone Lake.*